T0113308

WHERE FAITH ABOUNDS

True Life Stories of Love,
Death, and Faith

FRANCES M CHIOMA EBISIKE-EBOH

WESTBOW
PRESS®
A DIVISION OF THOMAS NELSON
& ZONDERVAN

WestBow Press books may be ordered through booksellers or by contacting:

WestBow Press
A Division of Thomas Nelson & Zondervan
1663 Liberty Drive
Bloomington, IN 47403
www.westbowpress.com
1 (866) 928-1240

ISBN: 978-1-5127-0287-3 (sc)
ISBN: 978-1-5127-0290-3 (e)

Library of Congress Control Number: 2016903419

Print information available on the last page.

WestBow Press rev. date: 04/06/2016

Contents

Dedication

To my Lord and my God who knew me before I was conceived in my mother's womb.

To Dad, Richard, who encouraged me with the powerful words "I see that God has put something special in you, take care of your siblings." Your words still echo in my ears till date. Adieu Pa!

To Mom, Josephine, my anchor; I owe my life to you and the peace you stood for. Adieu Mama!

Foreword

In this modern time people are inundated with news of death every day. Newspaper obituary pages and all media outlets are never bereft of chilling reports about it. A visit to hospitals, morgues, and funeral homes makes one come to terms with its realities. The bottom line, however, is that no day passes without news about death. Today, despite the fact that technology has led to advancement and improvement in so many areas of life, such as healthcare, food production, information, travels, recreation, and others people are still dying. That makes the age old saying that death is inevitable more real. No matter what we do we must die. One commentator says that dying is part of living. This is confirmed in Ecclesiastes 3:2 that there is a time to be born and a time to die.

Death has many characteristics, such as inevitability; is no respecter of persons; cannot be wished away; and others. Although it can bring closure or alleviation to some people especially the terminally ill and others whose conditions have become unmanageable, such as King Saul of Israel (1 Samuel 31:4), one common denominator is that death brings more negative than positive. It brings sorrow, mourning, anxiety, heartache, and all kinds of unbecoming conditions. Indeed, if there is anything people have worked tirelessly to prevent, it is death, but humanity is helpless with it. The lesson we should all learn especially when we pay attention to all the known people who have passed on despite their wealth, fame, and strength is that it is part of human existence. We should also remember that even Jesus Christ who Himself is God died but resurrected which sets Him apart from others.

Nevertheless, there are some who have felt the cruelty of death more than others. To such people mourning, fear, and hopelessness seem to be the order of the day. Sometimes it makes them ask why and wonder what is going on. This is the condition my beloved wife Frances the author of this book and all of us found ourselves. It became so incessant in the family that her supervisors at a point began to question her integrity suspecting that she was faking it to support truancy.

The benefit of all that she passed through, however, is that she has acquired so much experience and knowledge of issues about death and grieving that stand her in good stead to pass valuable information to people currently going through similar situations. Indeed, what she shares on the pages of this book are amazing and jaw dropping. They are so interesting that I found it difficult to drop the manuscript once I started reading it. Every page is unique with one interesting story and information or the other. A remarkable feature of this book is that Frances used storytelling technique and humor to captivate the reader. This is wonderful because people love to hear stories of other people's experiences to juxtapose with theirs in order to draw lessons. Another interesting aspect of this book is that it is not all about death. Frances took time to share many powerful and wonderful miracles that God performed in her life, our family, and others many of which I personally witnessed. That goes to show that even in the face of adversity God's mercy and love always reign supreme. This also confirms that God will never leave nor forsake His children (Hebrew 13:5).

Reading the manuscript of this book has been a great pleasure and I strongly recommend it for everyone as it can pass both for a religious and an academic masterpiece. The utility of what you will benefit by reading this book is worth more than the time and money you invest in it. God bless you as you read this interesting book.

Martins A. Eboh
Founder / Senior Pastor,
All Power Heritage Ministries Inc.,
USA & Africa.

Preface

Growing up, I was extremely emotional. One of the most difficult things I dealt with was news of the death of someone whether I knew that person or not. I would mourn and not eat. Sometimes I would be afraid and cry for days. I was fortunate not to have lost very close relatives at the time. However, I did not know that in future I would have to deal with incessant deaths around me. Never in my wildest dreams did I know that I could ever muster enough courage or have the grace to deal with such anomaly as I have seen people who mourn the death of their loved ones without any iota of hope some of whom have been completely devastated and their future ruined. I have also heard people talk about the fear of losing their loved ones and how impossible it would be to cope or deal with it. I believe that so many wrestle with such fear everyday. The reality, however, is that while some are in this situation there are those who have already experienced it and it becomes necessary to draw inspiration from them and, if possible, try to find out their coping secrets. That is exactly why I embarked on the long and tortuous journey to place this book in your hand.

The book tells my story; story of the myriad of deaths around me; story of life's struggles, uncertainties, and unwavering and unshakable faith. You will be encouraged and learn ways to prepare yourself and loved ones for the mystery of life and death that is beyond your imagination. You will learn about God's unfailing love and develop faith that will help you learn to persevere in the face of adversity. This book also shades light on grace and serves as a veritable tool in helping you and your loved ones know the love of God that leads to salvation and gives hope when a loved one dies.

A portion of this book, however, deals with my encounter with one of Africa's known atheists (who was also a relative) and what happened eventually. This is a must read. In this book you will be blessed by the catalogue of God's miracles that will not only "wow" your mind but also make you keep your mouth wide in amazement.

Moreover, this book was written with prayer accompanying every word and chapter. It is a glorious and anointed book. I believe that it will make a big and positive impact on you and your loved ones, and will also bring honor to our Almighty God.

May the Good Lord bless and keep you. May His love shine upon you. May God open your spiritual eyes to see and understand Him. May He do for you what human beings are unable to do for you. May the Lord help you understand His purpose for you. Most of all, may the Holy Spirit use the messages in this book to impact your life, the lives of your loved ones, and as many as will come across this book, in the mighty name of Jesus. Amen.

The portion of the scriptures below perfectly sums up everything you have just read, and I believe you will gain more revelation by the power of the Holy Spirit as you walk with me through the subsequent pages.

Romans 5:1-11, "Therefore, having been justified by faith, we have peace with God through our Lord Jesus Christ, through whom also we have access by faith into this grace in which we stand, and rejoice in hope of the glory of God. And not only *that,* but we also glory in tribulations, knowing that tribulation produces perseverance; and perseverance, character; and character, hope. Now hope does not disappoint, because the love of God has been poured out in our hearts by the Holy Spirit who was given to us. For when we were still without strength, in due time Christ died for the ungodly. For scarcely for a righteous man will one die; yet perhaps for a good man someone would even dare to die. But God demonstrates His own love toward us, in that while we were still sinners, Christ died for us. Much more then, having now been justified by His blood, we shall be saved from wrath through Him. For if when we were enemies we were reconciled to God through the death of His Son, much more, having been reconciled, we shall be saved by His life. And not only *that,* but we also rejoice in God through our Lord Jesus Christ, through whom we have now received the reconciliation."

Acknowledgments

My greatest appreciation and gratitude goes to my God who knew me even before I was conceived. Who lifted me up from the pit and put my feet on a solid rock. Who will never leave nor forsake me. Yes, to my God, my Lord, my Savior Jesus Christ who shed His Precious Blood for my redemption.

To my best friend, the love of my life, my husband, Rev. Dr. Martins Eboh who has always stood by me in trials and temptations. I cannot believe that it has been decades since I met you or rather since you sought and found me, the woman whom you now call "my beautiful wife." Thanks for devoting so much time reading and critiquing this book. I love you very much.

To my Honey Bunnies, my lovely children and prayer warriors Uche and Adaeze: I couldn't have asked for better kids! I love you s-o-o-o-o-o-o much! Though you are eight and four years respectively you are truly prayer warriors in the Lord's vineyard. Thanks for praying through every chapter of this book with me and declaring in your little voices that this book will be a "best seller" as it will reach the uttermost parts of the earth to encourage and bring people to the Lord. I know that God will answer your prayers. Amen.

To the one who deserves my appreciation, the unsung hero; the one that knows what I mean and what time it is; the one I call "Bro Sunny." Thank you for everything. I mean, e-v-e-r-y-t-h-i-n-g! Love and peace to you and your immediate family!

To my siblings, nephews, nieces, cousins, uncles, aunties, in-laws, and all extended family members from whom I have learned the importance of family and the joy in wrapping our arms around each other and savoring the benefits of solidarity and camaraderie. Together we will stand for ever. Amen.

To Aunty Virginia and Uncle Jonny, thanks for everything.

To Aunty Justina, thank you for your kind words during my days of adversity.

To Bro. Patty and Obioma, thank you.

To all the members of All Power Heritage Ministries; God bless you. I love you all but Jesus loves you more.

To my friends: Jessica Iwuala-Eben and family; Donald & Yvette Haughtons and family; Jewel Hall and Family;

Hillary Hall; Jodie Bonhnemetre; Cherrie Caccesse and family; Deola Agosa and family; Evelyn Pardallas and Family; Seonmee Lee and family; Nicole McFarlane; Veronica Short; Liberty Izevbuwa and family; Dawnmarie & Michael Rappaport. Thank you all.

To "Uncle" Artie Hartman, I love you very much. Thank you for everything. To "GG" Rae Hartman, you always told me how proud you were of me, and that really encouraged me a lot. You would have been proud of this book. I love and miss you. Rest in peace!

To the men and women of God who have dedicated their lives to the teaching and preaching of the Gospel of the Lord Jesus Christ: Pastor Russell Hodgins; Dr. Don Wilson; Pastor Sue Wilson; Pastors Dave Vandonge, Todd Clark, Mark Moore and the entire ministers and members of Christ Church of the Valley (CCV); You all are a source of inspiration to me. Thank you so much.

To Tonia L. Graham, NP; El-Mirage Family Health Center. Thanks for everything.

My gratitude also goes to the staff at Crossbook publishing, Mark Van Deman, Shaun Kauffman, Lauren Holmes, and others.

To you the reader who may have experienced loss of loved ones, or currently in the midst of it, or will experience it in the future I admonish and encourage you to please be strong, equipped, and prepared.

Dream Come True!

Dream Come True!

Although this book deals in large part with the issues of death and adversity, it is pertinent to start it in a lighter mood by highlighting and sharing some testimonies of God's love and miracle vis-à-vis a dream come true trusting that you will be encouraged as you flip through the pages. Before delving into the main themes, however, I invite you to share some of my experiences as a new immigrant to the United State of America (USA).

Coming to America was and is still a dream come true though in the beginning I had mixed feelings about it. Moreover, arriving in New York in the spring from a tropical climate I was really cold even though spring season is somewhat warm to some individuals. Many people wore light clothing and I wore winter clothes. The entire culture was also shocking and confusing to me. For instance, when I passed by people and greeted them in my usual good morning or good afternoon or good evening they would look strangely at me. I wondered why they were not responding to my greetings. Where

I was born people exchange greetings when they meet or bump into each other. I felt that people here were so busy with their lives that they hardly said "hello" to others.

Food was also different. I was used to eating organic and natural fruits, vegetables, and nuts freshly harvested from the farm; homemade spicy rice, beans, yam, soup, fufu and other African foods but here I was faced with what we would call snacks in my culture: fast food: fries, burgers etc. I missed my native food. I missed my family and friends. I missed home. Consequently, I took to writing down my feelings in form of poems, notes, and letters, and that was very helpful and consoling.

Apart from writing down my thoughts, some consolation also came from some of the materials I brought with me. For example, when I was leaving my mother gave me one of her wrappers (traditional cloth) which became one of my most treasured items. I used it to cover myself when I was lonely and cold. Sometimes I used it as a bed cloth. I hugged it when I missed home. Later I used it to carry my babies on my back. Funny enough, my husband used it to carry them too. Why is this funny? The simple answer is that in my culture it is only women that have babies strapped on their backs. However, because he struggled to do it as easily and perfectly as I did, I helped him out. He would carry the babies around the house and we would laugh and play. It was fun! Carrying my babies on my back with that wrapper (as it

4

is called in my culture) brought so much comfort, love, and peace to them. It was calming and would quickly and always send them to sleep while on my back. I also lent this wrapper to my friends and taught them how to carry their babies with it. I loved to do that. This cloth still remains a treasure and a significant part of my life till date. Years of usage have left it ripped and torn but it is still precious. It is amazing that it has also remained a source of comfort and love to my children even now they have grown bigger. Whenever they see it they feel cuddly and happy. They wrap it around themselves, hug, and ask me to carry them with it. "Uh, uh, you are now too big for it" I would tell them.

Nevertheless, during those early months in New York City, on Sundays as I went to church service, I expected to see almost everyone in the neighborhood going to church like it was the culture back home. Shockingly, the reverse was the case as most people went about their business just like any other day of the week. For the few who went their dressing was different and casual. In my culture people dress gorgeously and colorfully to church. They wear their best to go to the house of the Lord. However, I think either way is great as the most important thing is having Christ in us which is the hope of glory. I believe God wants us to come to Him as we are. Matthew 11: 28 (NIV), "Come to me, all you who are weary and burdened, and I will give you rest." I also believe that this applies to the fact that our body is His temple not our clothes; 1 Corinthians 6:19-20 (NIV)

"Do you not know that your bodies are temples of the Holy Spirit, who is in you, whom you have received from God? You are not your own; you were bought at a price. Therefore honor God with your bodies."

Another culture shocker was communication. Yeah, language was difficult with my "then very thick accent." Though I spoke English the accent was very different. People didn't understand me when I talked and I could hardly understand them either. I noticed that the harder I tried for people to understand what I said the more difficult it became. I was constantly faced with questions such as, "what did you say?" or "excuse me?" Also, the more people wanted me to explain what I was saying they harder for them to understand because then there were more words to figure out the meaning. What was a little helpful, however, was saying something and spelling it out. Non-verbal communication was also difficult for me as the gestures and signs here in the United States are different. Some are similar but mean different things. I recall at my first job the manager had waved "hello" to me. I went to her thinking that she was asking me to come. When I got to her she did not say anything. Then I wondered why she called me and did not say anything. The same way she waved her hand was the same way that we beckon someone to come to us in my culture.

Another culture difference was looking someone straight in the eye when in conversation. Here in

America it is the norm but in the culture where I was born it is seen as being disrespectful. You are supposed to look down when an elder talks to you, you do not look them in the eye.

How about the snow? My first experience with it was amazing. I had heard about and saw it in pictures and longed to see, touch, and possibly play in it. That fateful morning, as I came out of my apartment to go to work unaware that it was going to snow as I did not listen to the weather forecast, suddenly some white particles began falling on me. "Oh, all these dusty particles are all over me" I thought to myself. I wondered where they were falling from as I brushed them off my shoulder. As it continued, I noticed they were wet flurries instead of dusty particles. Then I heard passersby talking about the snow flurries. Immediately I became overjoyed to see snow for the first time in my life. I felt like rushing back to the apartment to call family overseas to tell them about my new find and snow experience, but I couldn't because I had to go to work. Later I told them and till date I still remember and relish that snow experience. I still love to play in it with the kids.

I have also had my own share of bullying and harassment. It took place when I was getting my citizenship. I had gone to the immigration office in New York City that day well prepared for my interview. As the examiner finished asking me questions, all of which I answered correctly, she requested to see my documents. After reviewing them her demeanor changed and she angrily turned off the voice recorder which she had initially told me would be turned on throughout my interview with her for training and recording purposes. With a frown and a very strong tone she said to me, ''you came here to this country less than four years and you now have a house and go to school at New York University?'' I became scared and started shivering. She then ordered me to bring a document that was not on the required list. With fear and the fact that I didn't know much about the law I promised her that I would. She instructed that I had only one week to bring the document or else I would be denied citizenship. She also instructed that if I brought it that I should look for her and never give it to any other representative. I agreed, and immediately I came out of the immigration office I called my family in Africa and asked them to send the document as quickly as possible. I prayed and trusted God, and within a few days the document arrived via courier service. I was overjoyed, and the following day I left for the immigration office to give it to her. When I got there and asked to see her, the representative I spoke with asked why I wanted to see her specifically. I told him that she had instructed that I give the document to no other person. He said that she was not available and that it should not have been requested because it was not on the list of items needed for the citizenship. I told him it was okay to still include it in my file. He took it and I left. I got my citizenship anyway. Hurray!! Instead of that immigration lady to commend me for my achievements she was upset. I guess she was being envious. Nevertheless, I thank God for His intervention. I believe God removed her from the office that day as she might still have come up with another missed documents story and probably denied me citizenship.

After graduating from New York University (NYU) I immediately got a job in New York City. Though I attended graduate school there it felt different working there. It was great and I loved it. It felt cool belonging to the class of "people that work in the city" from the Island. The commute was not bad. It was easier to take the city bus than driving so I took the bus as the bus stop was across the street from my house. It was fun and yet another culture of its own. New Yorkers "have their attitudes" they say, and you see that as you walk around the city or even at the work place. One day at work a co-worker said to me, "Hey! Where did you get your accent from?" I smiled and asked her jokingly, "Do I have an accent?" She frankly said, "Yeah, you do!" I said to her, "You know, you have an accent too." She was taken aback and seriously asked, "I have an accent?" Smiling and shaking my head positively, I replied, "Yeah, you do." "You know", I continued, "when I talk you hear my accent and when you talk I hear yours too because you speak differently from the way I do." After thinking about it a few seconds she said to me, "you are right, I never thought about it that way." We joked and talked about culture and how people see others different from them and things like that.

As an immigrant I see the United States as very lovely; the land of freedom; the land of care and compassion; the land of peace and joy; and the land that takes care of its own! My love overflows for the land that has become my land, my country, my USA. This is a country that values human life and fights for it; a melting pot of humanity where good deed is better appreciated, honored, and promoted, political and ideological differences notwithstanding. It is also a place of the good, the bad, and the ugly! A place I pray people will one day appreciate and serve God more in spirit and in truth for the love He has for them.

Wrapper from Mom. Adaeze cozy on my back (New York).

Wrapper from Mom. Uche with his Dad and
having a blast with it (New York).

Uche, Adaeze, and their dad playing in the
snow in front of our house (New York).

Adaeze, me, and Uche posing with the snowman
we made in front of our house (New York).

Snow Flurries outing. From left to right: Adaeze 3
years, my husband, and Uche 7 years (New York).

Snow Flurries outing. From left to right:
Uche, me, and Adaeze (New York).

"Because He Lives I Can Face Tomorrow"

"Because He Lives I Can Face Tomorrow"

A few years after I arrived here in the United States I got information that my father was very sick in Africa. My mother also had some medical problems but not as serious as Dad's. Adequate medical intervention was needed and by the grace of God they were able to join me and other family members here. Their treatment began as soon as they arrived. Sadly Dad's situation worsened. We were devastated. We prayed and trusted God. I was in school for my masters in social work, had two jobs, and simultaneously taking care of Dad and Mom. Indeed, all these were taking a toll on me. One day I was faced with so much work to do that I almost "lost it." I cried and cried and did not know where to start. With the daily treatment regimen of Dad, my two jobs, and piled up school work I was exhausted, lost strength, and wondered how I could continue with life the way it was. I recall walking down the school yard and wishing for any car to knock me down and kill me. For obvious reasons, I didn't want to take my own life. I was fed up with life. However, I trusted God and He intervened. Thank God for faith, the faith that He develops in us. We know that where faith abounds miracles happen. Faithfully holding unto God I was able to go to church where I always found joy, peace, and rest.

Meanwhile, that Sunday morning I was contemplating whether to go to church or just stay home to complete one of my nagging and overwhelming school assignments which I felt I would not be able to do when something inside of me said, "just go and God will see you through." I knew right away that it was the Holy Spirit talking to me. I went to church and sat down with my mind drifting from one issue to another. Just then Pastor Russell Hodgins, in his usual God-given beautiful and anointed voice began singing a song that I had heard for years which suddenly seemed new at that point, and it goes:

"Because He lives

I can face tomorrow

Because He lives

All fear is gone…."

Immediately I heard this song a cool refreshing blood ran through my veins. It felt heavenly! It was like I was hearing the song for the very first time in my life. I burst into tears and was silently saying, "Yes, yes, I can face tomorrow; because He lives I can make it; because Jesus lives I can do my school assignments, go to work, and take good care of Dad and Mom; because He lives I can live and not die; because He lives I can hold my shoulder high because I am a princess, the daughter of the Most High God." "Because He lives I can face tomorrow!"

At the end of the church service that day, I felt very happy, energized, optimistic, and confident that I would do well on my school assignment that I was to hand in the following day. By His grace I was able to complete it when I got home and happily submitted it in class the next day. When I got that particular paper back from my professor the following week my jaw dropped. I could not believe what was written on it. Not only did I get A+ my professor wrote "This is the best paper I have ever read, keep it up." Is it not amazing? Isn't my God good? Friend, it is wonderful what God can do when we obey and put our trust in Him. Proverbs 3: 5-6, "trust in the Lord with all your heart and lean not on your own understanding; in all your ways submit to him, and he will make your paths straight" (NIV).

Mom, me, and Dad (New York).

Expected Happening
At Unexpected Time.

Expected Happening At Unexpected Time.

As time went on Dad's sickness went on remission. He began eating and looking better and also began the process of completing a degree in law which was his passion. He loved to read and loved education. Dad loved education so much that he built a private Library in our compound (in Nigeria) so that we all would not have any excuse not to study. He had such unbelievable near photographic memory that he memorized one of William Shakespeare's books from cover to cover. Yes, Dad loved education to that extent! He also loved to teach. He and Mom started free adult education in our community in Nigeria. He taught one class while mother taught the other.

Mother who was always very helpful with Dad's activities of daily living despite her own ailments improved in her health too. I was very excited about their improvement. Dad and Mom also resumed their religious activities. They were truly religious, read their bibles daily, and devoted their lives to prayer morning, afternoon, and night. Church attendance and involvement were two of their and our most important family values. While he was in Africa Dad was very devoted to and began the first St. Anthony's Society in his then Catholic Church in the town. He and Mom were very wonderful people that loved and trusted God. What they lacked, however, was a personal relationship with Jesus. So we began to study the bible and not just read it. Eventually, after many years spent practicing church traditions and doctrines they truly began to understand the scriptures. They read John 3 over and over with emphasis on the dialogue between Jesus and Nicodemus. It was amazing! Please take a moment and read this beautiful dialogue:

John 3: 1-20

There was a man of the Pharisees, named Nicodemus, a ruler of the Jews:

[2] The same came to Jesus by night, and said unto him, Rabbi, we know that thou art a teacher come from God: for no man can do these miracles that thou doest, except God be with him.

[3] Jesus answered and said unto him, Verily, verily, I say unto thee, Except a man be born again, he cannot see the kingdom of God.

[4] Nicodemus saith unto him, How can a man be born when he is old? can he enter the second time into his mother's womb, and be born?

[5] Jesus answered, Verily, verily, I say unto thee, Except a man be born of water and of the Spirit, he cannot enter into the kingdom of God.

[6] That which is born of the flesh is flesh; and that which is born of the Spirit is spirit.

[7] Marvel not that I said unto thee, Ye must be born again.

[8] The wind bloweth where it listeth, and thou hearest the sound thereof, but canst not tell whence it cometh, and whither it goeth: so is every one that is born of the Spirit.

[9] Nicodemus answered and said unto him, How can these things be?

[10] Jesus answered and said unto him, Art thou a master of Israel, and knowest not these things?

[11] Verily, verily, I say unto thee, We speak that we do know, and testify that we have seen; and ye receive not our witness.

[12] If I have told you earthly things, and ye believe not, how shall ye believe, if I tell you of heavenly things?

[13] And no man hath ascended up to heaven, but he that came down from heaven, even the Son of man which is in heaven.

[14] And as Moses lifted up the serpent in the wilderness, even so must the Son of man be lifted up:

[15] That whosoever believeth in him should not perish, but have eternal life.

[16] For God so loved the world, that he gave his only begotten Son, that whosoever believeth in him should not perish, but have everlasting life.

[17] For God sent not his Son into the world to condemn the world; but that the world through him might be saved.

18 He that believeth on him is not condemned: but he that believeth not is condemned already, because he hath not believed in the name of the only begotten Son of God.

19 And this is the condemnation, that light is come into the world, and men loved darkness rather than light, because their deeds were evil.

20 For every one that doeth evil hateth the light, neither cometh to the light, lest his deeds should be reproved.

21 But he that doeth truth cometh to the light, that his deeds may be made manifest, that they are wrought in God...

Another portion of the bible that ministered deeply to Dad was 1 Corinthians 7:14 "For the unbelieving husband is sanctified through his wife, and the unbelieving wife is sanctified through her believing husband; for otherwise your children are unclean, but now they are holy (NIV).

This scripture impacted him so much that he said he wanted to live up to it. He decided that if he made himself right with God our entire family would benefit from it. He decided he would give himself to God to save his family. That was remarkable. I loved and appreciated him more for that. A man giving up his life for his family! Wonderful!

Dad, Mom, and I continued studying the bible together and if I needed any clarifications, being a young Christian at the time, I would call my then fiancé and now husband. It was wonderful and great. Dad and Mom were doing great so life was sweet though I still had to go to work and school with all the stress involved. Eventually, one day Dad accepted Jesus as his Lord and personal Savior and got baptized by Pastor Hodgins at the International Christian Center (ICC), Staten Island New York, USA. It was one of the happiest days of my life. We celebrated and dined with friends. Dad said he felt glorious. It was a glorious day indeed! Heaven and earth rejoiced! I will forever cherish the memories of that day which was also captured on photos and videos. It was amazing! Dad was extremely joyful and grateful to God and never wavered. On the other hand, Mom continued her belief in God, prayed a lot, and continued to read the bible but was unable to give her life to Christ till a couple of years later. Moreover, Dad was a very humble person. I recall one day he knelt down seven times in the living room asking God and us his children for forgiveness if he had offended us and others. I was very touched. I begged him to get up and reminded him that God is such a merciful God that immediately you ask for His forgiveness He answers and that he didn't need to kneel down seven times to obtain forgiveness and mercy. I used that opportunity to reiterate to him and Mom what wonderful parents they had always been and that they never offended us. I guess Dad was making sure there would be no sin found in him when he would stand in the presence of Almighty God on the appointed day. Besides, he had advised me to let his friends and family members know about this.

As we know, life is a roller coaster. Sadly, Dad's sickness returned. I was devastated. I fasted and prayed, our church ICC prayed, family members prayed, friends prayed, and I begged God to please, please heal him and not take him away from us. I told God how important Dad was to our family and his community in Africa. How life would come to a standstill if he was no more. I prayed with many scriptures and reminded God of His promises to those that believe in Him. My favorite prayer scripture was Isaiah 38: 5 "Go and say to Hezekiah, 'Thus says the LORD, the God of your father David, "I have heard your prayer, I have seen your tears; behold, I will add fifteen years to your life" (NKJV). I begged God to add fifteen more years to Dad's life.

As I prayed and prayed the Holy Spirit began to minister to me about appreciating who Dad was and what he did. As the days went by my prayer focus changed. It shifted from what I wanted God to do to appreciating every single day that God allowed Dad to live with us. I began to appreciate the fact that God gave me such a loving Dad. I thanked God for the wonderful parents He gave me and my siblings. I celebrated every moment and it really helped to prepare me for the more difficult days to come.

During Dad's sickness, one of the movies that remarkably brought joy to us was "The Sound of Music." I wrote a poem about it thus:

Lasting Impression!

It was a sound so gentle to my soul.
A sound that made Dad's pain go away and stopped him from wandering about.
A sound that made him sound like himself again, telling Mom and I what happened those days of Hitler.
A sound that reassured us that Dad's memory was not totally gone.
A sound that brought laughter to his mouth in the heat of "after-radiation" pain.
A sound that made Mom sit down and watch TV leaving the dishes on the dinner table for the first time in years.
A sound that made us happy.
It was the sound of music!

Lasting impressions I call thee!
Therapy I call thee!
The sound of new life you are.
You are the sound that made me sit and think.
The sound that drew me even closer to the little ones.
The sound that helped me face my problems rather than run from them.

The sound that helped me believe that whatever will be will be.

The sound that helped me remember that children have the heart of Jesus, but turn out to be what you make them; that they love before they hate while adults hate before they love.

The sound that reminds me to love and care.

The sound that makes me want to have two sons and five daughters.

It was the sound of music.

God bless your heart Maria for leaving these lasting impressions on us all.

For making us remember that music is for the soul and love is from God and prevails.

What would I have done in a weary evening without you my sound of music?

Though you are old you are the newest thing in my life!

If I had no name I would have loved to be called "The Sound of music" so that everywhere I go I brighten people's hearts.

But since I have a name I will keep you close to my heart so that each time I move; I will hear a little sound that will renew my spirit and then I will share it with others.

Oh! My sound of music!

The sound so real and true."

One day Dad told me that he had something very important to tell me. I was very nervous. Was he to tell me he was going to die? With my heart beating so fast I managed to hide my tape recorder so that he could not see it in other for him to be totally natural in his speech. I recorded everything he said including his goodbyes. It was a powerful moment. The truth from his heart echoed in that room that hour followed by tears, silence, and other emotions. Dad knowing later that I recorded the conversation was very happy and grateful that other family members would be able to hear what he said. In later conversations with him he would request that they be recorded or videotaped.

Nevertheless, on that fateful day the expected happened at an unexpected time. Dad was called home to heaven. The day began as any other day. Nothing unusual or extraordinary was expected. As I was getting ready to go to the hospital that morning to relieve mother so that she could come home and freshen up I was led to read lamentations 5:3, "We are orphans and fatherless, our mothers *are* as widows." I wondered why I would be led to read that. It was surreal. I was still trusting God to heal Dad so I didn't think of him dying that day or any time soon. When I look back now I realize how the Holy Spirit was always leading me through and preparing me every step of the way. Also prior to his passing, I had a dream where he was lifted up to the heavens. In this particular dream he was lying in something that looked like a recue stretcher (not medical stretcher that has wheels) and was lifted up in the air into the cloud.

That was another revelation of what was to come, and still in denial, I did not try to understand it.

Though we all expected it to happen one day we didn't anticipate it that day. However, Mom had told me several times that when I was away at work Dad would tell her that he was dying and she would question why he would decide to die when I was not around. He would assure her that when the time came that I would be there, and he did as promised. Mom and I were standing beside him when he breathed his last. Watching that happen was the worst experience in my life and the memory has stayed with me since then. Not being able to stop death was devastating. At that time I cried and begged the doctors to bring him back to life. I asked them to put him on life support with hope that with prayers he might miraculously come back to life. The doctors and nurses tried to revive him to no avail. Dad, my precious Dad, my role model was gone and gone forever! I recall running out of the hospital room into the elevator, knelt down, and began to beg God to please bring him back to life. Other passengers on the elevator graciously held me and tried so much to console me but I was inconsolable. Immediately the elevator stopped I ran out to inform Bro. Sunny who was standing outside with Dad's friends that visited from another state. They too were devastated and quickly ran upstairs.

I was grief-stricken as my life had turned upside down. I lost my dearest Dad, my best buddy. He was the center of my world. How could I live? How could I live without him? What was I going to do with my life? How could I console my mother and siblings? How would I tell other family members? How would I tell my siblings, uncles, aunties and other extended family members overseas? How this …how that…. Memories flooded my brain. H-e-y! Can anyone understand my situation? My heart was broken! I was sad and scared. Happiness eluded me. Nothing mattered anymore to me. People were like dim figures. My world had fallen apart! How could I ever be happy again? What is the point of life? Life is useless! Life is meaningless! Life is nothing! At this point a thought flashed in my mind that Dad was at peace!! Another thought said, "no, but he could still be at peace here with us." Meanwhile Mom was very sad and scared too. I felt so terribly sad for her because she came to the United States with her husband and would soon be going back to Africa without him. What a life!

Coming back to the apartment after Dad's passing was horrifying. It felt so empty without him. However, I guess, I was in denial as I felt as if he was still alive. I felt horrible as I constantly thought that he might have woken up in the morgue and was struggling to come out. I felt like I should call the hospital to go check on him. I thought several times that he might call me to come pick him up from the morgue. Mysteriously, however, a couple of times during those few days my phone would suddenly ring and I would rush and grab it thinking that he was calling me to pick him up. It was weird that each time I picked up it would go dead on the other end. Sometimes I asked Mom if she also heard the phone ring or was I just imagining it? She would confirm that she did hear it. Mystery? I don't know. Days that followed were miserable but for love and encouragement that came from friends, immediate and extended family, and our dear church members at International Christian Center (ICC). I remember a church member say to me without even knowing so much about Dad, "Your Dad went from glory to glory." God really used them to wrap His arm around us and provided some comfort.

At the final viewing before Dad's body was flown to Africa for burial Obi told the mortician that the hinged side of the casket was pressing down on Dad's leg and respectfully asked if she could pad it or do something so that it would not hurt him. The mortician looked at him and firmly said, "he is dead, it is not going to hurt him." That caring statement by Obi has lived with me for all these years. It goes further to show how we view our loved ones even in death. When it happens, at first we are in shock, we don't accept it even if we are seeing the lifeless body lying in front of us. How can one possibly accept that one will never ever see one's loved one again forever? It is very hard and difficult.

My husband who was in Africa when Dad passed told me how he ran into a friend who started telling him a story about a wonderful man from the neighboring town that had passed away in the United States and how his towns people were mourning him and many saying that their lives would be meaningless without this man. When my husband told him that the man he was talking about was his father-in-law the man was shocked. My husband also told me that when he went to the village to deliver the news about Dad's death that some old and young people were crying uncontrollably. Many of them were throwing themselves on the floor (a practice of deep mourning and show of deep sadness in my culture) and saying that their world had ended because they had lost the only one that cared and advocated for them. That's exactly who Dad was. He touched so many lives. He would give his last meal to a hungry man. He led his community even from his sick bed thousands of miles across the ocean. A mighty man he was. Dad and Mom single-handily built homes for the very poor in the community. They cared for theirs and other people's children that sometimes people could not differentiate between their natural and foster or neighbor's children. They shared everything they had with people in the community, namely, food, medicine, clothing, and many others. I believe God rewarded them for all these by making it possible for them to be saved. My fondest memories of their generosity were during Christmas time when Dad and Mom would buy gigantic bags of different kinds of food and we would put them in smaller bags and give to poor people in the community who didn't have much to eat or celebrate with.

Nevertheless, despite all my pain following his death I still wanted to love God and tell people about Jesus. I received the Christian orientation that we have to be faithful to God and serve Him with all our heart whether in pain or happiness because He is a loving God and will always be with us. I knew without a doubt that God in his infinite goodness was keeping me strong. I was experiencing an inner strength that was unimaginable. Something inside me was keeping me strong and I knew it was the Holy Spirit. While on the plane heading home to Africa for the burial, Mom sitting by my side, I was giving out tracts to people and telling them about Jesus. It felt good lifting up the name of Jesus in that situation. By the grace of God we arrived safely in Africa and a couple of days later Dad was buried. The burial ceremony went well as thousands of people came and paid their last respect. There was plenty to eat and drink while the people celebrated their hero.

Night After Dad's Burial; God's Name Glorified

Praising the Lord and giving Him honor despite anything going on around me has always been my forte. The night after Dad's internment, armed with strength that could only come from above, I had the opportunity to tell people that slept over at the house about Jesus. After my testimonies thirty people confessed and received Him as their Lord and personal savior. How awesome God is! However, prior to Dad's passing and while praying for him I believe that God was saying to me, "My daughter I have my plan for each and every one of you, I care about your father's eternity more than his ephemeral earthly gains; though I prolonged Hezekiah's life it is okay for your father who is also my son to join me now because whether he lives or dies he belongs to me." Romans 14: 8: if we live, we live for the Lord; and if we die, we die for the Lord. So, whether we live or die, we belong to the Lord. God continued to whisper in my spirit, "I will use his death for my glory." The salvation of many people that night, I believe, was a confirmation of this. Dad impacted so many lives before and after death and continues to do so to the Glory of God Almighty. No wonder the scripture says in Psalm 116: 15, Precious in the sight of the Lord is the death of his saint. Dad's death also confirmed the words of Paul that "for to me, to live is Christ and to die is gain (Philippians 1:21). I am so glad that Dad became born again and eventually made it to heaven. It is amazing that the last words he wrote on his diary before he went to be with the Lord were about his baptism. After writing he kept the red pen he used on the same page and it has been there till date. It has become a memorial.

I Loved Her So Much And She Is No More!

My younger sister Uchechukwu (meaning God's will) went to be with the Lord at a young age. Two weeks before she died she called me from Africa and we had discussions about certain things. She also expressed regrets about some of the things that happened in her life and asked for forgiveness. She reached out for reconciliation with family members and wished things were different. We prayed together over the phone and we encouraged each other. After our conversation I asked her if she would like Jesus to come into her life. She responded "yes." I led her through the salvation message and prayer and she accepted Jesus as her Lord and personal savior. She did! Yes, she did! About two weeks after this remarkable communication with her I received the shocking news of her death. Everywhere and everything seemed dark just as when Dad died! Another heart break, another pain, another sorrow! It was not easy for me but I was consoled by the fact that she accepted Jesus as her Lord and personal savior.

I was also encouraged by the fact that God used me to lead her to Christ. Then came the word of God to me in Proverbs 11:30, "The fruit of the righteous is a tree of life; and he that winneth souls is wise" (KJV). These words from the most important book in the entire universe made my faith grow like a colossus!

About a year after her death my son was born. I was excited that God had broken the cycle of sorrow and mourning in my life. My husband and I greatly rejoiced as this was our first child and agreed that we would name him after my late sister for my love for her and also for her encouragement before I got pregnant. Although we demonstrated this unflinching and unwavering love I still feel sad that she died and her death broke my heart. Thank God she got saved and is in a better place. How glorious it will be the day we will meet with the Lord to part no more as declared in 1 Thessalonians 4:17, "Then we who are alive and remain shall be caught up together with them in the clouds to meet the Lord in the air. And thus we shall always be with the Lord." Hallelujah!

**Beyond Mother Lies, I
In Misery And Agony
Holy Spirit Intervened.**

Beyond Mother Lies, I In Misery And Agony, Holy Spirit Intervened.

When I was going back to United States after Dad's burial Mom refused to come back with me and other family members. She felt happier in the land she was born and bred. She stayed in the house with her maids and would visit with my sisters from time to time. They all enjoyed having her. I would call and speak with her as often as possible. When my sister Uche passed away she was heartbroken. Africans believe that children are supposed to bury their parents and not parents burying their children. However, the birth of my son brought some consolation to her. She was even happier knowing that he was named after Dad and my sister. Mother was not able to see my son Uche due to distance. I would call her and have him babble in her ears which she enjoyed and cherished. I also made pictures of him and sent to her. I tried updating the pictures as Uche grew older and would send them to her. Long distance communication with Mom continued until that day we chatted and I remember promising her that we would be coming to visit her soon not really knowing that that was our last conversation. Two days later my sister Berna called from Port Harcourt where Mom went to spend time with her and her family and reported to me that she was in coma at the hospital. Words cannot describe my grief and despair. I could hardly believe that such could happen to my mother whom I recently had a wonderful conversation with. In the days that followed I would call and have them put the phone in her ear so that I could talk to her and pray for her and tell her how much I loved her. I also told her that my son and I were planning to come and see her in a week or two. I quickly started getting our travel papers together.

However, a couple of days later I received the dreaded call, a call that still lingers in my memory till date, a call I wish never came, a call that snatched the phone off of my hand and smashed it into pieces on the wall. This is a call that no one would ever want to get; a call that said that Mom was dead! Being heartbroken was an understatement. I could not eat or get out of the room for days. I did not accept it. I cried till I lost my voice. I did not care about life any more. Life meant nothing. Everywhere and everything seemed dark again. The world seemed empty and useless again. One does not get used to losing a loved one. Never!

As I said earlier, when I heard that mother was in coma I began getting my travel papers ready. I prayed none stop and trusted God that she would come out of coma before or when I got there. However, when the news of her passing came I refused to believe that she was actually dead. I rather believed that she was in coma and would wake up. I actually bought clothes and shoes for her to wear to celebrate her coming back to life. I trusted and prayed and believed. I had to go to the immigration office and got all of our documents ready. My son and I left for Africa about two weeks after she passed. We got there safely and into the warm and loving embrace of my siblings, their families, and other extended family members. It was wonderful seeing all of them but very sad that Mom was not there. Though she was in the morgue I continued praying and trusting God that she would wake up to the surprise of everyone. It did not happen. During the viewing I was so overwhelmed with grief and expectation that I actually felt that her body was literarily moving and that she was waking up. Even till she was interred I still kept trusting and believing that she would wake up from the "coma." To my greatest disappointment she never did! I began having doubts and mixed feelings about God. Is God truly real? If He were, why could He not answer my prayers? Why would a loving God allow my mother to die? I had prayed and quoted all the scripture verses I knew none stop, trusted, believed, prayed, and prayed and prayed. I had reminded God of His promises again and again; reminded Him of how He raised Lazarus as well as the young man from our town who died, was put in the mortuary, and came back to life after many days.

Why did He not raise Mom the same way? I reminded God how humble, loving, and giving mother was. Being from a Royal family she never let that get into her head. She believed in the equality of everyone and extended her royalty to all. She trained all of us the same way and we also never allowed our royal privileges influence us. Indeed, God allowing mother's death to happen made it difficult to trust Him anymore.

Nonetheless, the night after Mom's burial, I was miserable and in much agony. I lay on the bed, could not sleep, crying my eyes out, and asking God why? why? As I meditated, however, the Holy Spirit began to minister to me and told me how mother prepared her life for heaven before she died. I heard a voice ask me a question: "would you have preferred to have her come back to life and misstep or would you prefer that she made it to heaven without any scores to settle?" I said, "I prefer that she made it to heaven." Right there and then my healing began. I felt peace come over me. I was once again reminded of Romans 14: 8, "whether we live or die, we belong to God." As faith flowed into me again I was able to go to sleep afterwards. In the morning I gave the shoes and clothes I had bought for her to family members.

I am thankful to God that while Mom and Dad were here on earth I was able to eat with them, read with them, cry with them, sing with them, write with them, worship with them, and be there at Dad's passing on behalf of my siblings that weren't around. Today when I look back at my life I thank God for giving me the opportunity to share my sincere thoughts and love with my parents as expressed in the words below which I gave to them in form of a card when we were together.

DEDICATION TO DAD AND MOM

Father and mother, sweet and strong
Your hearts, full of love and tenderness
Lay on the altar of your hearts, beauty and loyalty
By your sacrifices, beauty and goodness
you have made the world fairer
For these I give you my blessings

All through the years, you have served the world with dedication
Years of joys and sorrows
Years of love and care
You labored faithfully, truthfully, and fruitfully.

To you father and mother
Fond and true
I give my love and pledge of loyalty
In the alter of my own heart
I light a candle for you that will forever burn with love.
You did your part for us all
You have a special place in my trusting heart
A love that will forever be.

I looked up to you for my daily bread and
You offered your life to give it to me
You were loyal as well as faithful.

Without your guidance I couldn't stand
I honor you both
Accept my treasure of love
A treasure so sweet and true
Meant for only father and mother like you.

The word of God, the Bible in Ecclesiastics 3:12 says, "To everything there is a season, and a time to every purpose under the heaven. A time to be born and a time to die…." Friend, is this a time to live for yourself? A time to live for God? Please choose this day to live for God. You will have no regrets. My Mom and Dad led lives worth emulating; life of love, care, and service to God and man. Mom and Dad shared their love and possessions. They both touched so many lives in positive ways. Most of all they lived and died in Christ. They both gave their lives to Christ. To God be the glory! I still remember with nostalgia the folk song the people of the community composed and sang about them and in their honor many years ago: translated in English thus:

"When you reach the tip of the street,
you will see the light, the only light in the town.
The light that has brought joy and happiness,
and made us belong like the rest of the world.

The light from Richard and Josephine.
We thank and honor you."

Prior to mother passing, however, she went to everyone she felt she had issues with and made peace. She advised us to live peaceably with all human beings as the bible commands in Romans 12:18. That is the advice of a true woman of God. Like my husband rightly pointed out, "your Mom died like a woman of God that she was." As related by my sister, on that fateful day, Mom went to a Christian church near their home, worshiped God, made herself clean before God, came home, said her prayers, finished her dinner, and slid into coma from which she transitioned to eternity to be with the Lord. I am always amazed whenever I remember her end of life events. The night following her burial, immediate family members, extended family members, and friends converged and powerful prayers were offered and people made resolutions to God. I am so proud of the life my dear mother led. "For to me, to live is Christ and to die is gain" (Philippians 1:21 (NIV). Adieu Mom! Adieu!

No one could have eulogized Mom better than Aunty Virgy did on the "masterpiece" below:

"MRS JOSEPHINE EBISIKE MEMORIAL LECTURE....

Late Mrs. J. Ebisike, ...was the joy of this family, and was loved by all. Since a year ago, we have not heard from her which means, she has gone forever and the vacuum she has created in this family can never be filled by any other person. She was a woman of vision, honor and worthy of emulation. She made sure that her impact on this earth remained forever. She made it a must that her natural and foster children, and also others around her got good education, at least first degree. What a wonderful achievement! She has given us the greatest gift anybody could give to any child. We are really proud of her. She saw what this information age would bring, while others were sleeping. And she laid the foundation for us.

Throughout her short stay on earth, she stood for peace, love, education and reconciliation. Shortly before her exit; she went round, sowing the seed of reconciliation. The greatest honor the women of Okponkume and Mpam should give her is to emulate her by giving their children proper education in order to eradicate illiteracy in our midst.

It is only education that will liberate us. The question of apprenticeship is old and obsolete. It is of agrarian mentality. Make sure you and your children form the habit of reading. Read everything. There's no limit to what you read because you never know where you will get the information or idea that will liberate you and lead you to the world of abundant wealth. People don't like reading. They only want money, forgetting that the right information required to make the money is written somewhere. We need information. Information is ruling the world. To break the shackles of poverty and flourish in this our world of abundant wealth, you need the right information and better ideas.

Things have changed and will continue to change. For you to be part of this change, you need the right information. Let's look at the three most significant ages that have passed this world of ours and see how people faired in order to appreciate what I am talking about.

The Three Most Important ages:

1. Agrarian Age
2. Industrial Age
3. Information Age

In the agrarian age, the rich were those who owned castle and fertile agricultural land. They were the monarchs and the nobles. If you were not born into these two groups or not there by marriage or conquest you were powerless. That age's wealth creation was popular, respected, and handed down from generation to generation.

Then came the Industrial age and wealth shifted from agriculture to industries, factories, buildings, mines etc. These were placed on top of agriculture. The value of land dropped because wealth shifted to the owners of buildings on the land. The rich fertile land became less valuable and rocky land suddenly became more valuable. People built skyscrapers on them. The net worth of farmers went down. Their standard of living dropped. At that time those who went to school and got the right education became very rich and powerful. Entrepreneurs who started with nothing became billionaires. They were respected and worshipped. They had great wealth and power and their standard of living went up. They were only very few of them and we were not there. Now, comes the information age. The big question is, are we going to be there? Your answer is as good as mine.

THE INFORMATION AGE. Our own Age: The World Wide Web (www), the scientific cloak around our world, has changed what it takes to join the rich class. You don't need to be of a noble birth or royal family as in the agrarian age or to be an entrepreneur before you will become very wealthy. What you need is information or bankable ideas to become very rich. In this information age, it does not really take money to make money. What it takes most at times is idea. Bring out one idea or make an old idea better and you are on top of the world. The Greek Philosopher, Democritus said: "Rather would I discover one idea than be the King of the Persians." He did find many ideas. Really, ideas need not be new. They just need to be better and sellable. Rich people are always looking for better ideas. Bill Gates did not invent the operating system that made him the richest man in the world for thirteen years. He only bought the system from the computer programmer who invented it and then licensed the product with IBM. Now, the rest is history. Lots of people are now billionaires before 40. Where are we? Do you want us to be brushed aside in this age? During any economic bonanza, there are only three kinds of people: Those who make things happen, those who watch things happen, and those who say: "What happened?"

My dear young boys and girls, where will you belong? The decision is now not tomorrow. Mrs. J. Ebisike helped to flower and water this age for many including you all here now. This Lecture is a part of her horn of plenty. Let's start to reap the fruit of her labor.

Our age's Internet has made it possible for more people to use their ideas and create assets that buy other assets and have their financial dreams come true. You can choose to live in a world of poverty or that of plenty. The choice is yours. Go ahead. Make your choice. Good luck!

Mrs. Virginia Ebisike-Etim."

"What A Gift She Gave You"

About a month after my family and I moved to Arizona I went to volunteer at a hospice care agency. During the interview one of the supervisors explored with me what my experience working with hospice clients, dying, and loss was. After telling her how I was present alone when a hospice client passed away she said "what a gift she gave you." I was shocked. I never saw being present at that client's side when she passed away as a gift. I was horrified as a result of that experience, I had nightmares, and my fears worsened everyday. As was my agency's protocol, however, I had to clean the dead body, dress it up, call 911 (police department), and alert the agency management. When I think about it now, I agree that that experience really made me stronger. During this meeting with the hospice supervisor she went on to say that the client was comfortable enough to share that moment of exit with me. Really? Wow! "I never saw it that way," I told her. She said that from her experience some people would make sure that everyone left the room before giving up the ghost, and in other cases they might want someone they trusted to be there at that point of exit. She went on to say that that client felt comfortable enough to have me there as she exited the world. From my own experience I have seen that people's death desires are different depending on their circumstances. One experience is always different from another. However, an important question is how do we prepare for death when we do not know when it comes? It is simply by accepting Jesus as our Lord and Savior. That way our eternity with Him is guaranteed. Hebrews 9: 27, "And as it is appointed unto men once to die, but after this the judgment:"

Luggage Ready Heading For The World Beyond

My mother in-law Irene about one year prior to her passing prepared herself for the heavenly journey. She gave instructions to some important people in the family about what to do after her passing, the need for them to live in peace, how to take care of vulnerable members of the family, who should inherit which property of hers, and many other issues. However, my husband not knowing that his mother had plans and had prepared for the world beyond travelled to Africa to see her and other relatives. On the eve of his travel we phoned my mother in-law and chatted with her. I asked her what she wanted me to buy for her. She jokingly said that she wanted me to get her "fried chicken and other kinds of meat in America." We laughed about it and I told her that I knew the kind of things she liked and would get them for her.

On getting to Africa, my husband spent some quality time with her and made sure that he bought her fried chicken and other food that she enjoyed. According to my husband they spent time reminiscing and talked about many things as she was very excited. About two days later, while he was out visiting with my sister Uk, he got a call from her that he should come immediately and quickly because she needed to talk with him. My husband hurried back to her. During their conversation my mother-in-law, a woman of God, told my husband that she had "made ready her luggage" and had been waiting to see him all these years before passing on. My husband was shocked but just managed to record their conversation and appreciated every moment of it. One striking and remarkable aspect of their discussion was that she was very excited about going to be with the Lord and to, according to her, "join others to praise God and shout hallelujah." While he was still there in Africa my beloved mother-in-law, a God fearing and loving woman, who always fondly called me "Chioma nwam" (Chioma my daughter) went to be with the lord on March 4th of that year which coincides with my daughter Christa's birthday. She really made sure that her memories lived on because each year my daughter's birthday is celebrated we will always remember her in a special way. When I thought about it I felt that that date was remarkable; that she had urged us to march forth (March 4th) despite anything going on around us. As painful as her death has been my husband is always consoled by the fact that God gave him the opportunity to see her again after many years he had not seen her. **"J**esus said unto her, I am the resurrection, and the life:

he that believeth in me, though he were dead, yet shall he live" (John 11:25 (KJV).

What an awesome experience! It was really a miracle that he went to see his mother because he did not intend to travel that year. He was into his first year of internship for a master of social work (MSW) degree when he was suddenly and unceremonious withdrawn from a program he had already put in many months. At first he was very disappointed and upset. I thought about it and as usual went to God in prayer. I found out that God wanted to use it for His glory. I also remembered Romans 8:28, "And we know that all things worketh together for good, to them that love God, to them who are the called according to his purpose" (KJV). To this day my husband blesses the Lord for allowing that disappointment whenever he remembers that God used it to give him the opportunity to see his mother before she passed on. God is miraculous and will always order our footsteps when we make Him Lord and the center of our lives. When one door closes God opens another beautiful one. When we are faced with disappointments and failures in life we should surrender all to God who has greater plans for us. God always sees the future and what we do not see.

In The Bossom of the Lord

Prior to and after my mother's passing we had other deaths in the family. This became so incessant that it became an issue at my job. My supervisors began to suspect and whisper that I might be faking or exaggerating it. I did not blame them for their suspicion because it was really bad. No six months passed without a report of death in my family. I prayed and asked God to stop it. However, the passing of my little nephew was another dim and grievous moment of my life. Everywhere and everything seemed dark again. Why would God allow my handsome baby nephew to die? And why did He make him so special to me and then allow him to disappear from my life? My special connection with this baby began December 31, 2001 about 8:35 am. While praying for my family the Holy Spirit revealed to me that my two sisters (Norah and Bernadine) were pregnant. In that revelation I was given a specific month for the birth of Norah's baby which was July. I later confirmed that they were truly pregnant. I prayed for them and waited. On July 29th there was no news about the birth of the baby. I became anxious and started questioning if the revelation I got was really from God. I began having the feeling of disappointment because it was two days before the end of July and the baby was not yet born. I waited for the news and did not get it. I went to sleep. The following morning, the morning of July 30th, I was awakened by a phone call and my sister Norah gave me the good news of her baby boy's birth. I was overjoyed and praised the Lord whose words never come back void. He was named Chiebuka (meaning, God is great). A couple of months later, I travelled to Africa and was able to carry him and my other cute nephew Obinna (Daddy's Pet) who was born a couple of months later in my arms. Ebuka as we fondly called him was every babysitter's joy. He was charming, ever smiling, and never fussy. I made sure I took several pictures and videos of him and other relatives before heading back to the United States. It felt great looking at those pictures over and over and watching the videos. Unfortunately, a couple of months after I came back I received the dreaded call that Ebuka had passed away. I was devastated and mourned for this precious baby. When I spoke with my sister Norah and her husband I was surprised to hear how strong they sounded. They were rather consoling me. Deep down I knew it had not been easy for them. I thanked God for giving them such grace and fortitude to bear the loss of their only son. Such strength could only come from God.

I have come to realize that we are only caretakers of children. God owns them. We only take care of them for

Him because we are just "renters" (parent = pa---rent). Whenever they have their final rest with God we should take courage in the fact that they belong to Him and not us. It is not easy and will never be but in such times God will surround us with His Spirit to minister peace to us. Psalm 127:3, Behold, children are a heritage from the Lord... (NKJV). We take courage that to be absent in the body is to be present with Christ (2Corinthians 5:8). I thank God that Ebuka is in the bosom of the Lord.

A Loss So Deep!

The loss of my husband's beloved younger sister Charity was unimaginable. It was unbelievable that she died so suddenly. She visited home after many years of absence and the family celebrated. My mother-in-law was very excited to see her. Her son whom she kept under the care of the eldest brother was very elated to see her too. My husband worked very hard to see that she made that visit irrespective of her reluctance and several postponements. I remember how happy we were to speak with her. Like I indicated it was unexpected. Have you lost a loved one unexpectedly? Have you suddenly received a message that someone you least expected to die was dead? It is heart wrenching. It is unfathomable and brings a lot of sorrow. This is the mood we found ourselves when the news came that Charity was dead. I was having fun at the park during our Agency Family Fun Day when that call came. In his anguish my husband went straight to the point, "Charity is dead," and broke down. His heart was broken because he loved Charity so much. I was also heartbroken and quickly left the party for home to be with him. We were considering different ways to help get her established before this and all had to come to an end. The sad reality is that we were not sure if she received the lord before her death. I spoke with my mother-in-law and other relatives and was consoled by how strong they were. Till date my husband and I still miss her. We wish she did not die. We continue to take solace in the word of God and continue to pray against untimely death in our family.

Isaiah 57: 1, "Good people pass away; the godly often die before their time. But no one seems to care or wonder why. No one seems to understand that God is protecting them from the evil to come" (NLT).

Dark Moment, God's Reality

Another dark moment was the untimely death of my beloved brother-in-law who as the husband of our eldest sister played a central and strategic role in our family. Will my sorrows ever end? Why will the God I love so much allow all of these to happen to me and my family? I began to have some unbecoming thoughts: If He were a true loving God and loved us why would He take our loved ones and leave us heartbroken again and again? Maybe my uncle who was an atheist was right. Maybe there's no God after all! Maybe we human beings created God instead of God creating us as the atheists say? May be I have been tricked into believing that there is God. There was nothing to believe anymore! Nothing! However, I am convinced that no matter what there is God and the answer and proof is right there in the bible and in most of the events and things I have experienced in life. Yes, God is real. Please make out time to read the bible and meditate on it as the Lord has commanded in Joshua 1:8, "This book of the law shall not depart out of thy mouth; but thou shalt meditate therein day and night, that thou mayest observe to do according to all that is written therein: for then thou shalt make thy way prosperous, and then thou shalt have good success" (KJV). Paul also admonishes in 2Timothy 2:15, "Study to show thyself approved unto God, a workman who needeth not to be ashamed, rightly dividing the word of truth" (KJV).

As a result of all these deaths in my family I have searched and searched for answer as to why good people die early and the wicked live longer! Have you ever asked such a question? I have asked this over and over again. Recently, as I began to pray and meditate and ask the Lord about this the Holy Spirit took me to Isaiah 57: 1, "Good people pass away; the godly often die before their time. But no one seems to care or wonder why. No one seems to understand that God is protecting them from the evil to come" (NLT). To a child of God who is grieving the loss of loved ones this is a wonderful consolation. This is a precious gift from God to you. Please be encouraged and cheer up.

Heaven Is Our Home, Earth Is Just A Temporary Place We Pass Through.

Imagine when a child leaves home for another state or country how the parents long for him or her to be back. When he / she finally returns they are excited. It is just the same with God. He is our father and heaven is our home. The world is a temporary place. Our home is in heaven with God. Jesus says in John 14: 1-3, "Do not let your hearts be troubled. You believe in God; believe also in me. My Father's house has many rooms; if that were not so, would I have told you that I am going there to prepare a place for you? And if I go and prepare a place for you, I will come back and take you to be with me that you also may be where I am" (NIV). That is why this song by Jim Reeves resonates with me:

This world is not my home,
I'm just a passing through,
my treasures are laid up,
Somewhere beyond the blue…."

Yes heaven is our home and earth is a temporary place. It's like relocating from your birth place to another state or country. There will always be the hunger to go back. As I mentioned earlier, when I newly came here to America I missed home so much that I wrote:

HOME SWEET HOME
Home is where I long to be
Home is where my heart belongs
I long to be with friends and families
Home brings memories to me
Memories of my life, God's love and protection
Home is where it all started
Home, you are my root, my life, my joy, and my happiness
Home sweet home I am desperate for you!

Home sweet home
You are full of nature
Every plant I see reminds me of you
Every flower that glows smells like you
Every song I hear draws me closer to you
Every moon that shines opens my heart to you
Every sun that sets feels like you
Home sweet home, I cannot do without you.

I wish I can fly
I wish I have wings
I wish I am a bird so that I can fly home

Home sweet home, you that would have been the best place to live in the world,
you that is rich in natural resources and great in climate,
Home sweet home, the great gem of Africa,
Home sweet home the giant of Africa,
Home sweet home, I long for you and I want to come back to you.

Home Sweet Home
As I cry for you and long for you,
I am scared to come to you,
I pray for you, the Land that is full of corruption,
The Land that is full of injustices,
the land that is full of disrespect for women, especially,
The land that suppresses education,
The land that promotes evil and devalues worthiness
Your youths are scattered, they cry out to you: to be heard, to be better to live and not die.
Home Sweet home!! Home Sweet home!!!

Home Sweet home
I pray that the hand of Almighty God may reach you.
That the Lord God may one day let his light shine upon you and deliver you,
That one day, the world will know and hear and then my God will intervene and deliver,
While I am away and long for you, I will hide myself in prayers for your deliverance from all the forces that have pervaded you my home, my land.

Though you are rich in natural resources, you have become poor due to your rich selfish rulers, who smash the head of your young ones that try to raise their head to save others;
True democracy will one day reign, as God will intervene and deliver.

Home Sweet Home,
I have a promise to you
To pray without ceasing for you
To live my life to uplift you, 'cause you bare me, and 'cause good can still come out from the bad.
As I wait to come back to you
Again, I will do that which will uplift you,
I will love, and help, and serve,
I will pray and pray and pray and wait till the hand of God overtakes you.
I will forever acknowledge you my home, my old world, my Nigeria, my Africa and yet embrace you my new world, my future, my America.

Though I still miss my birth home I understand that I have another home, the heavenly home, where I will meet my loved ones one day to part no more. I believe it is a better place, a place where no earthly possession is allowed, a place of no worries and stress. That is why all the fighting, killing, and maiming that this world is associated with are vanity upon vanity. Do we really realize that when someone dies he or she leaves all his possessions behind? I mean everything. This world is not our home indeed! Why worry when we have a better place in heaven? "But our citizenship is in heaven. And we eagerly await a Savior from there, the Lord Jesus Christ" (Philippians 3:20 (NIV).

In The Realm of Humanism and Atheism the Power of God Manifests

In The Realm of Humanism and Atheism the Power of God Manifests

When uncle Eze or Dee Sylve as we fondly called him passed away I was very sad and heartbroken. Death! Death! Death! Everywhere I looked it was like death was there knocking. Will this ever stop? Will dying ever cease? This is a man known around the world, an ex-Roman Catholic Priest, former President of the Nigerian Humanist Movement (NHM), a renowned atheist, a jovial friend to many, father, grandfather, uncle, and author of over 29 books. Death indeed is no respecter of persons. A couple of years ago I began an e-mail correspondence about God and being born again with him. I invite you to share some of my e-mail communications with him and also see the power of God thereafter:

On May 5, 2009 I forwarded an e-mail to Uncle Eze titled "60 seconds with Jesus." This mail had the story of Jesus and quotes from the bible.

His scornful response is interesting. Please pay attention to the title of his response: **"a wasted effort, say I"** and rather than greet me appropriately he angrily used my e-mail name which is an English translation of my native name.

Date: Thu, 21 May 2009 04:51:20 -0700a
Subject: Re: FW: 60 secs With Jesus ...**a wasted effort, say I**.
To: goodluckf@hotmail.com
CC: ....

Hi Goodluck Frank,

The story (Tori) of Jesus is a story told by idiotic 419ers. It's like W. Shakespeare wrote, full of fury, signifying utter stupidities. To try to prove the historicity of your dense Jesus is like an ostrich that hides its head in the sand and thinks it's hidden.

Jesus is a fictional character whose molders forgot to put into his silly 'logias' - sayings a thank-you to Africa that saved his Hebrew race from starvation and saved him from the haunt for slaughter by Herod and to his mother and all women. It's said that he shouted at her : ' Woman, what have I got to do with you?' Had such degrading disregards for women that made him not to marry any but preferred to use them for his mean selfish ends. What an ingrate's your Jesus!! A lying bigot who called us infidels. Do I list the lies here? Not now please!

Do something else. Don't waste your precious time on inanities, trapped inside a *cul de sac* . Please get out to the sun shine of those who know how the world works.

Cheerio to you and yours!

Eze Ebisike, former Chairman of Nigerian Humanist Movement, a concerned world-citizen.

Wow! that was a "biggie." Please take a deep breath and patiently read my response to another email:

goodluck frank <goodluckf@hotmail.com> wrote:

Hi Uncle Sylve,

It's always a pleasure reading your mails. Here's my suggestion / reaction(other reactions may follow later):

As we remember Mom and others this period, may we also remember what she stood firmly for: belief in God. This belief in God has become who we are, and we cannot write our history without it. We can't even live without it. May God help us. In writing our history, please do not forget that God is our base. It is part of the reason we are what we are today, and it has been molding us. We are the symbol of religion or Christianity in our town. During mom's burial…, the officiating Priest couldn't have said it better when he pointed out that there would be no Christianity in Okponkwume without Ebisike's family, in which Uncle Sylve, you played a big role. I believe it's part of the reason you are what you are today. I have come to admire you a lot. I'm proud of you. You are full of knowledge and wisdom. You are loving, caring, always sharing, very pleasant, very accommodating, patient and very sincere. I sincerely love to read your write-ups, which are knowledge based. You are impacting "our" world in so many different ways. However, I must be sincere to let you know that sometimes, I don't agree with some of the things you write, especially, about God. I believe that God is real. He is real to me; and I have experienced his power and might in so many different ways. His ways are not our ways. He is loving, faithful and true. He is the God who is "able to do exceedingly and abundantly above all we ask or think." (Ephesians 3:20). He has been everything to me. He is also our comforter, our strength, our hope, our joy, our peace, our redeemer, our all in all. He is the living water from heaven, the ancient of days, the resurrection power, the bright and morning star, the everlasting God. The God that forgives sins. He is the reason for my (our) living.

Uncle Sylve, I urge you to reconsider and make JESUS CHRIST THE LORD of your life and he will never leave nor forsake you. Believe on the Lord Jesus Christ and thou shall be saved and thy house (Acts 16:31). Please read also the following; John 3:3,16; Acts 4:12; Isaiah 55:6; Hebrews 9:27. My prayer is that the good

Lord will bless you and have his truth shine upon you. May you accept him as your lord and personal savior. May others do so too. Amen.

Uncle Sylve, I want the best for you. My prayers are always with you, your immediate and extended families, our clan and our people in general.

My regards to your beautiful family.

Love you.
Chioma.

Please check out his response to the above; now he calls me by my native name not my e-mail name.

Date: Mon, 21 Jul 2008 12:47:54 +0100
From:
Subject: RE: The Memorials and First Draft of Our History... Your lovable comment in focus
To: goodluckf@hotmail.com

Hi Chioma,

You are a great preacher, dear Baby ! Hearty congrats indeed! Your suggestions to improve Our History in the making are Ok. We will make a better job of it by up-dating it unconditionally and continually. More power to your able elbows. How are you and yours, especially your lovely bubbling baby? We are ok here!

My only comment on your sermon on Deus, Deities and the abominable book, the Christian Bible, indeed any religious bible is to tell you to do a good reading of any work on:

i) Form Criticism of the bible

ii) Textual Criticism of the Bible.

After that, I will recommend other works that you will consult.

The biggest recommendation now is to ask you to read at least four books on any subject even children's books every week and within a year, you will regret your religious position today.

Reading is the food of the brain. It's the revolutionalizer of the mind. Every starved brain harbors the religious deadly virus. The believer's God-delusion is a reality that is non-illusion. Your President, born-again, God-deluded Bush Jr. is a typical example of what a prominent non-reader's tragic life-stance and danger to his/her neighbor and the world can be.

Religion is nothing but insanity and Karl Marx was right in Religion is the opium of the people. I can't improve on that now.

But I must admit that your expressing your conviction so forcefully gives me a great pleasure. Keep it up. You will make an astounding humanist like the Nobel Laureate, Naine Gordmer of South Africa, when you receive the eye-&- mind-opener that comes from reading the readables and unreadables through avidity in reading.

Greetings to all ...there.

Tell Eboh that I'd love to hear from him. Does he know how to preach like you?

Cheerio to your son.
Eze.

Wow, he is advising me to read some of the works of people criticizing the bible. Food for thought: if he believed these works, why would he not believe the bible? Well, anyway, I wrote again:

From: goodluckf@hotmail.com
To:
Subject: RE: The Memorials and First Draft of Our
History... Your lovable comment in focus
Date: Sun, 27 Jul 2008 20:37:54 -0400

Hi Uncle Eze,

It's always a great pleasure hearing from you. I get excited whenever I read what you write. Thanks for considering including our "Christianity" in the draft of our history. It means a lot to us. I encourage you to keep it up. You are doing a great job; it will be remembered forever.

I must confess that through the years, I've learned that great reading / knowledge is great vexation. No wonder King Solomon, whom I am sure, you believe was once a king in ancient Israel, said in Ecclesiastes 1: 18, "For in much wisdom is much grief: and he that increaseth knowledge increaseth sorrow." The solution to the problem of man does not depend on the number of books read, rather wisdom from God. I also believe, Uncle Eze, that we human beings are always searching for peace, happiness and a feeling of fulfillment: these do not also come from reading. I suggest that no amount of reading should dissuade one from the truth, the bible, the word of God. God is love, peace and wisdom!

May I quickly react to your statement about my born-again President: the bible teaches that it is not always good to put people down, especially those in leadership positions. I try to give honor to whom honor is due. I believe that God has all of us here on earth for different reasons. Mr. President is in his post for a reason, so is any one of us; and God will use us any how he wants. I would like us to remember that nobody is perfect. Perfection can only be found in God.

Uncle Eze, may the good Lord bless you and keep you. I will continue to pray for you. Please do not forget, John 3:3, "...verily verily, I say unto thee, except a man be born- again he cannot enter into the kingdom of God"; also John 3: 16 says, "For God so loved the world that He gave His only begotten son that whosoever believeth on him shall not perish but have everlasting life." This is a choice you will not regret. God loves you so dearly. He has a wonderful thought (plan) for you, (Jeremiah 29: 11) God wants you to spend eternity in heaven by believing in the lordship of Jesus Christ. Please read Romans 10: 9, 10. I love you and your family very much. I love our clan / our people. I pray that everyone makes it to heaven.

My husband, Martin, sends his regards. You may hear from him soon as you requested. We are doing very well here, to God be the glory. My son, Uche, is growing into a very handsome, strong, energetic, bubbling, cultured, prayerful boy. I thank God for him. We are truly blessed and highly favored of God.

I hope to hear from you soon, Uncle Eze. I must go now, because Uche is tugging me to play with him. My sincere love for your family and our Clan. My prayers are with you all.

All my love!

From his Vineyard,

Chioma.

Uncle Eze wrote:

Date: Wed, 30 Jul 2008 14:24:58 +0100
From:
Subject: No! No! No! Dear girl
To: goodluckf@hotmail.com;

Hi Chioma,

Greetings to you and yours from us here! It feels good and cool to hear that Uche is doing marvelously well like Uwaoma who's starting to crawl and eats us out of house & home.

You were at your best element while you were saying your say here. An excellent exposition of expressing one's conviction. But your homily on religion, on buffoon Bush Jr. as Europeans and many intelligent people across the globe see him, and on the impossible plagiarized work, your Bible.

1. No religion is higher than love and truth. Indeed it's about hate and 3Ds... Danger, destruction and early death. Every religion is about God-delusion. If it's worth more than 'hell is paved with good intentions,' I would have known it years ago. Do understand that I was one of the best and brightest clerics that ever came out from Africa then. When I discovered the great flaw in all religions I had to resign from the bottomless pit that is religion.

2. So tragic a person as Bush Jr. could only be chosen as a President by a place with corruption-ridden religion. Here's your President: His grandfather was a Senator, his father is an Ex President. He was more than once the Governor of Texas where he signed more warrants of capital punishment than all the other Governors' put together in order to stop crimes in Texas. Did he, before or after he left it for the presidency, stop criminals there? Answer that for him! As a President he was inspired by his dearest Jesus to see axis of evil nations he would decimate one after the other. Your President does not know whether Nigeria is a country or a Continent. He does not know whether Africa is in Nigeria or vice versa. During three Debates he had with John Kerry, he did not pass even one. In his earlier debates with Al Gore, he had only one pass. Today humanist Al Gore is a Nobelist, a Nobel Laureate, a member of the world's

core-elite, a position he and 99.999% of all believers can only be in their nightmares and insane visions. This your wonder-God has no redeeming feature at all or else he would have allowed the USA to have humanist Al to be President; to share the glory of Australia or China where humanists are ruling today.

3. No! No! No! Dear Girl! No! Solomon did not write the Ecclesiastes. Neither him nor his father wrote anything in your dense Bible. Nor did Moses write the Pentateuch.

If you did read any sensible work on Texctual Criticism of your Bible, you would have known that Aesop of Ethiopia, an atheist wrote the Ecclesiastes. His other works make that obvious He was the world's greatest fabulist, the counselor of the world, my mentor.

One of the evil effects of interpolations of the so-called writers of the bible and Patriarchal Patristic fathers of the Church did the deceptive tragedy that led you & billions to conclude that those Agrarian kings wrote any part of the bible. And the Constantine's stupid Council of Nicaea in 325 selected the 72 or 73 books they called the bible. They never thought that our generation would unveil their stupidity. St Augustine of Hippo (Algeria) confirmed the madness. Just as he made their Jehovah, Deus from being called a Deity Just as he created Heaven and Hell, as He made Mary Queen of Heaven, as he created Original sin of Adam and Eve, etc. It's St

Augustine who destroyed the world with mad Doctrines that all religions upheld to the damage of believers' minds and aspiration to be honest humans.

Hence every believer is always looking for what lie to tell about anything and has always something to hide, always afraid of something. Always prefers good intentions to good deeds.

Don't forget that I don't believe in anything. My knowledge of the world is enough for me. Belief or faith debases every believer's ego and destroys the fight in it.

Write more to me, I beg you!

Cheerios to you and Martins and bubbling Uche.

Eze Ebisike

It was very upsetting to me that Uncle Eze poured vituperation against the president simply because he professed to be born again. Did you notice the level of anger he exhibited in this e-mail?

However, I wrote him again:

From: goodluckf@hotmail.com
To:
Subject: RE: No! No! No! Dear girl
Date: Sun, 10 Aug 2008 17:18:47 -0400

Hi Uncle Eze,

I'm glad to hear that Uwaoma is doing great. I believe that his Maama is doing well too. My regards to them and your big boys.

Uncle Eze, do you know one of the reasons I love you very much? You always try your best to encourage one despite the circumstance. I believe you will make an excellent evangelist. Nothing is too late, you know.

In your last mail you stated, "Do you understand that I was one of the best and brightest cleric that ever came out from Africa then." Uncle, not only do I believe you were. I do believe that you are still one of the best and brightest beings I've ever known. Please never allow people's flaws and errors deprive you of the love of God.

Uncle, you remind me of Apostle Paul, in the bible. May Almighty God forgive you as he has forgiven me and others; and may he restore you fully for his kingdom. Amen.

Please do not forget, John 3:3, "...verily verily, I say unto thee, except a man be born- again he cannot enter into the kingdom of God"; also John 3: 16 says, "For God so loved the world that He gave His only begotten son that whosoever believeth on him shall not perish but have everlasting life." God loves you very much.

I will continue to pray for you, your family, and our Clan.

All my love!

From his Vineyard,

Chioma.

There were so many other emails we exchanged some of which might not be relevant in this book. An interesting one, however, was the one he emailed asking for my and a couple of other folk's critique of his 30th book that his publishers were refusing to publish. He did not care that I might not be in agreement with the content. He wrote:

Date: Fri, 10 Oct 2008 14:16:25 +0100
From:
Subject: Your critique and or criticism of the following Please!
To: …goodluckf@hotmail.com;….

Ladies and Gentlemen, October 10, 2008

A happy day!

I have contacted you because of your specialty. And I respect your judgment and expertise. Below is my response to Prometheus Books publisher's rejection of my MS: 'Visions 20 In 2020 and Homicides In 2050'. It's my 30th book. May I identify you to the others? You are eight ladies and seven gentlemen as follows:

….Chioma, a liberation-biblical theologian — African-American….(other names deleted by me).

Please do advise me on what you think of my presentation before I will send it to the Editor-in-chief of Prometheus Books soon. You are free to let the others know your reaction or only to yours truly,

Eze Ebisike.

I was honored to be asked to critique his response; however, it was not something I was passionate about so I responded:

From: goodluckf@hotmail.com
To:
Subject: RE: Your critique and or criticism of the following Please!
Date: Sun, 12 Oct 2008 18:43:19 -0400

Hi Uncle Eze,

I always admire your strengths, openness, courage, enthusiasm, etc. Congratulations on the amount of knowledge you have put out there to the world. 30 books- great achievement indeed! I hope they reconsider their decision and help publish your book.

Good luck and God Bless!
My love to your family.
Chioma.

Nevertheless, some interesting things about Uncle Eze are that he was very soft minded and loved people. He was also very brilliant, educated, handsome, and charismatic. He was and still is a symbol of Christianity in his community. His father (my grandfather) was also the symbol of Christianity as he established the Catholic Church in the community. When he died he was buried inside the church to honor him. As you can see I had a wonderful communication with Uncle Eze in my bid to bring him back to Christ. Indeed, he seemed impossible to accept the Lordship of Jesus. However, the events that took place after will shock you!

About a couple of weeks before Uncle Eze passed away at the age of seventy-five I spoke with my beloved Aunt Virgy who was caring for him. I asked her if I could speak with him fearing he might not make it. My intension was to further tell him about the love of God and the need to be saved. My Aunt sorrowfully told me that he was not able to talk as he was very ill. I was very sad because I did not want him to spend eternity in hell. I remember getting into my car after speaking with my aunt that afternoon and seriously cried out to God for him. I recalled the beautiful song that was sung by the town's people to honor Uncle Eze and Ebisike family which in my native language says:

"Ekechala fada na mba na mba oke ahaghi otu,
a Chukwu ewere fada Ebisike nye anyi
ndi Mpam obodo anyi emepele."

(Translated in English, thus: "Priests have been distributed all over the nations, God knew that it has not reached us and gave us Priest Ebisike, and now our town has seen development.")

This is a testimony of the love of the community for this man at the time, and I trusted that the Lord would on that basis see him through. As I always do I prayed and left everything in God's hand being consoled by the fact that I had tried my best to tell him about Jesus. Sadly, a couple of weeks later he passed away. I was disappointed that this "good" man vehemently rejected Jesus as much as I knew. This broke my heart as I also missed him. For months, I wondered if he in any way thought about God during his sick days and if he changed his mind and received the Lord. Then came the big surprise!

About seven months after his passing I was having a phone conversation with my sister Norah when she mentioned that it was remarkable that Uncle Eze accepted Jesus eventually. I could not believe my ears. I asked her to repeat what she said and she asked me, "did you not hear what happened the day he was buried?" and I responded, "No, what happened?" My sister went ahead and told me how after all the Humanists gave their speeches and before he was lowered into the grave a preacher came up and gave testimony about how she ministered to Uncle Eze and he became saved and accepted Jesus as his Lord and personal Savior. My sister said that after that testimony the atmosphere changed. Their mourning turned into joy and they went about rejoicing. I screamed for joy and began to praise God. What a great news! Uncle Eze of all people confessed Jesus? How awesome that is! How gracious our God is! Who would ever believe that an atheist, a humanist, and former chairman of Humanists who was highly respected in Africa and beyond would ever come to the Lord? It is the Lord's doing and it is marvelous in our eyes. I prayed and trusted the Lord for the salvation of my uncle and God answered me. Thank you Jesus!

For you dear friend praying and seeking the Lord for your family members or loved ones to be saved please keep praying and trusting God for in due season He will do it even at the last minute. Also, you that are sad that your loved one died without Christ do you know whether he or she received Him without you knowing?

What really gave me joy about Uncle Eze's salvation stems from knowing the grace of God and the power of forgiveness. When I was a teenager he lived in the city of Lagos Nigeria. I longed so much to visit there as friends and relatives who went came back and told beautiful stories about it. Uncle Eze gladly welcomed my siblings and cousins who wrote and asked to spend holidays with him. They also came back and told beautiful stories about their experiences. I wrote and asked to visit him but to my greatest shock and consternation he bluntly refused. He wrote me back that "I will be the last person to invite you to my house." I was shocked, disappointed, embarrassed, and sad. I wondered why an uncle I loved, respected, and cared so much about could treat me that way. I agonized and cried so much about it that my sister Norah consoled me and vowed never to visit him herself. She was so sweet. I carried that disappointment and hurt for years wondering why he would write such a letter to a young, delicate, very responsible, loving, and beautiful niece of his. However, when I became born again I was able to forgive him and everyone that had hurt me as the love of God was shed abroad in my heart by the Holy Ghost (Romans 5:5). In one of my visits to Africa, I gave him gifts and some money not necessarily because he deserved it but just to show him the love of God in me. I responded positively several times he asked favors from me. At the back of my mind, however, I always wanted to ask him why he wrote that letter to me but I never had the opportunity to do so. Indeed, I am always made strong by the Word of God that "…It is more blessed to give than to receive" (Acts 20:35 (KJV).

Nevertheless, I believe that God did not want me to make that trip to Lagos else He would have allowed it. I have learned that He has always been in control of my life and will allow things to happen as He pleases. This gives me a lot of consolation. That is why when things do not happen the way I plan them or someone denies me something I do not take it personal as God may be using that situation to do something in my life or save me from unnecessary inconveniences or trauma. Who knows if my uncle allowed me to visit him I would have died in a car accident thus destroying my destiny and hindering the work of God I am currently doing. God will always protect and order our footsteps if we put our trust in Him.

Uncle Eze's story reminds me of a similar story of my friend's father who was also an atheist. This man vehemently refused to acknowledge God till an event in his life led him to change his belief. To make a long story short, he became saved after he had a terrible auto accident and saw the abundant mercy and grace of God. Years later he died assured of a secure eternity. I believe that there is something about dying that makes people want to get it right with God. Some people do have the opportunity while others unfortunately do not. Please make it right this moment and you will never regret it. "Seek ye the Lord while he may be found, call ye upon him while he is near: Let the wicked forsake his way, and the unrighteous man his thoughts: and let him return unto the Lord, and he will have mercy upon him; and to our God, for he will abundantly pardon" (Isaiah 55:6-7 KJV). Amen.

"Mommy, I See A Doctor's Book and A Bible, Can I Have Them?"

My three year old daughter, Adaeze, had been saying that she wanted to be a doctor since age two. Initially, she said that she wanted to be a pastor because that was what his brother said he wanted to be. Then one day she changed her mind and said that she wanted to be both a doctor and a pastor. She asked me if she could be both. I told her that she could and that it's only God that would give her the strength and wisdom. This does not seem to be a typical conversation of a three year old. Amazingly my daughter and I do have mature discussions, and sometimes, I say to myself, wait a minute, she is a toddler, not even a teen yet. To the glory of God, she is very bright and mature for her age. God has given her lots of wisdom and I praise Him for that. I recall when she was a baby, not even crawling yet, that whenever I chewed something, she would put her hand on my chin. She would feel it and watch the jaw move back and forth. She still does that occasionally and is very detailed in her observation and analysis of things.

She always checks things out and plays "doctor" and "pastor" with her favorite doctor's toy kit. She loves bible stories which she looks forward to before she goes to bed every night. I am sincerely grateful to God that at three years old she reads at a 5th grade level. To God be the glory and honor. For years I had dreamed, prayed, and trusted God for intelligent and God loving children and I am grateful that He answered me.

Moreover, whenever Ada sees a book about doctors or bible she would grab them and start reading. One day, we went to the El Mirage Fire station for an event-Christmas toy drive, pancakes, and Library book sale. After she and her brother had given their toy donation which they had prepared weeks before the event, we had the opportunity to meet with the wonderful Fire Fighters and Police, beautiful and humble El Mirage Mayor Lana Mook, and Councilman Roy Delgado. Beautiful people in El Mirage I would say. After, we headed to the Library book sale section and while we were going over the books Ada said, "Mommy I see a doctor's book and a bible, can I have them?" I responded, "Yes, I will buy them for you." She immediately started reading them while his brother, Uche, was on the other side going over other books. Reading is Ada's forte. An older Lady came and admiringly said to her, "I see you love books and you can read?" She nodded in agreement and immediately said to the Lady, "hm, your face is very small." The nice Lady agreed and said, "Yeah, I have a small face." I was shocked and embarrassed. I cut in and said to her, "yes her face is beautiful too." Kids, sometimes, can be impulsive and say things as they are. However, the lady's face was truly smaller than normal but very beautiful. She asked my daughter if she did go to church seeing the religious book she had. She said "yes." The Lady told her that she belonged to a church too, and she smiled, had a couple of more discussions with the lady and continued her reading. Meanwhile, the lady and I introduced ourselves to each other, chatted about church and her relocation from California to El Mirage, Arizona. I also told her that I had recently moved from New York. She said that she and her husband felt very blessed because of improved economic situations, a more beautiful house, and that she attended a beautiful church close by. She expressed great faith in God and talked about how wonderful He had been to her. One of God's favors, according to her, was her daughter getting saved before she died. She said that her daughter had become sick and passed away shortly after. She happily said that she knew that her daughter was in a better place in heaven. I admired this woman's faith in God in the midst of adversity. I feel so happy when I see people expressing this amazing happiness that comes with knowing that their loved ones made it to heaven. Later on, however, she introduced her jovial husband who had been busy collecting books. We chatted a little more with them and departed.

I think about this Lady often. What great faith she had. I admired her coming to terms with the death of her daughter. We met by chance and it was amazing how a simple discussion with my daughter led to my being availed the opportunity of hearing her beautiful story and her conviction and peace with God. If not for this conviction she and her husband, I guess, would have been depressed due to the loss of their young daughter but instead they happily accepted her death knowing without a doubt that someday they would meet her again to part no more. Jesus is the healer of our soul and body. There is always peace that comes with accepting the lordship of Jesus over our lives. The world we live in can be cruel, hash, and condemning, but with Jesus you will always have peace and confidence no matter what life brings your way.

Personal Growth, Lessons Learned, And Advice

Death Is Inevitable!

It does sound like I have had lots of death around me. True! Guess what? Death is a necessary end that will always happen. If you have not experienced it in the past, my guess is that you are experiencing it now, or you will experience it one day. Death is inevitable. We cannot run away from it. It is part of life. It happens sometimes without warning. When that happens to your loved one, my advice is, take heart and be encouraged. Our heavenly father will send his Angels to wrap their arms around you and console you. As long as you put your trust in Him He will never leave nor forsake you. God does feel our pain. In Psalm 91:15 He says He will be with us in trouble. Notice that He did not say He will stop our troubles or take them away. That means there will be trouble someday but God will be there holding our hands. In the midst of our afflictions, in the midst of our sorrows, in that time of crises, it is very difficult to see or sense God's presence. It is usually later on when we reflect back that we usually see how present God has been around us and in our circumstance.

Through my personal tribulations I have been able to acquire some personal attributes and skills, such as, greater spiritual growth, patience, compassion, empathy, loyalty, love, to mention but a few. I still have trials and testing, and it's okay because I know, that I know, that I know that my God is ever present. The world is full of trials, temptations, and struggles but our God is ever present and always there to see us through. I have also come to realize that God is more concerned about our eternal bliss than our earthly welfare. In recent years when something happens in my life my reaction is always that God allows it to happen for a reason and He will be with me, He will see me through. Sometimes I see the reason immediately and sometimes afterwards. I will always be grateful to God for whatever comes my way. God does bring good out of every circumstance. For example, following my mother's death family members agreed that every year, during Christmas time, everyone including extended family members would gather and celebrate life and achievements instead of gathering only when there is death or crisis. Till date this gathering has been taking place every Christmas and the purpose of bringing all relations together has been achieved. This has also benefited other people in the community as Aunt Virgy and her husband whom God has blessed the community with and whom I call the "Oprah of our town" provide different humanitarian and philanthropic services such as, free medical care, free community development projects, free giveaway, quiz competition and prize winning events for young people, etc. It is amazing how tragedy can be turned into triumph and it takes prayers and faith in God to make that happen. Kudos!

September 11, 2001.

On September 11, 2001 the world witnessed one of the horrifying events of our time in the United States. That day, coordinated terrorist attacks were launched against our nation in New York City and Washington, D. C. by Islamic terrorists known as Al-Qaeda. According to news reports as captured by Wikipedia:

Four passenger airliners were hijacked by 19 al-Qaeda terrorists so they could be flown into buildings in suicide attacks. Two of those planes, American Airlines Flight 11 and United Airlines Flight 175, were crashed into the North and South towers, respectively, of the World Trade Center complex in New York City. Within two hours, both towers collapsed with debris and the resulting fires causing partial or complete collapse of all other buildings in the WTC complex, as well as significant damage to ten other large surrounding structures. A third plane, American Airlines Flight 77, was crashed into the Pentagon (the headquarters of the United States Department of Defense), leading to a partial collapse in its western side. The fourth plane, United Airlines

Flight 93, was targeted at Washington, D.C., but crashed into a field near Shanksville, Pennsylvania, after its passengers tried to overcome the hijackers. In total, almost 3,000 people died in the attacks, including the 227 civilians and 19 hijackers aboard the four planes. It also was the deadliest incident for firefighters and for law enforcement officers in the history of the United States, with 343 and 72 killed respectively.

I recall heading to Brooklyn by bus for a training that morning of September 11 and seeing the World Trade Center in smoke. There was fear, mourning, sadness, despair, and hopelessness pervading the entire landscape. It was not God's will that thousands of lives, homes, business, and others be lost; and yet the atrocity was committed in God's name. These individuals and their group reported that they did it in the name of God. They meant evil but it was amazing what came out of it- out pouring of support for one another, love, charity, and kindness. The Fire fighters, police, paramedics, and others who sacrificed their time, health, and life to rescue and help others will never be forgotten as they wrote their names on the indelible sand of history. We know that the God we serve gave all humans free will. Unfortunately, the terrorists chose to use theirs to destroy and thank God many resorted to use theirs to love and care in that time of loss and sorrow.

For me that day began as a normal day. I woke up early in the morning, said my prayers, handed my life to the

Lord, and had my usual cereal breakfast before catching the bus to Brooklyn oblivious of what would happen later. By the grace of God I was able to get to my training location at Marriot Hotel in Brooklyn. The training was later cancelled because of the pandemonium and chaos that ensued from the attacks. The streets were overcrowded. There were mourners everywhere, and many people were confused not knowing what to do or where to go or how to get to their families. The air was filled with smoke as sadness pervaded the landscape. It felt like the world had come to an end. Movements were restricted as Police blocked roads for security reasons. One had to show one's identification to even get to the next street. I felt trapped at Marriott hotel where the training was to take place and unable to go back to the Island where I lived. My co-workers and I though scared and heartbroken immediately became volunteers, donating blood and helping with one task or another as the hotel was turned into a place of refuge for individuals. Hall ways and rooms were all crowded with people. Some were dejectedly sitting down, some exhaustedly lying down, and many were standing wherever they could find space. After hours that seemed like eternity we were given pass to go home. Back on the Island, though a few miles from New York City, I was still able to see the smoke from my then 4th floor apartment. Words could not describe how horrible it was. I was exhausted and unable to eat because there was no appetite. I went on my knees and began to pray for our nation and all who were affected by this wickedness.

It was interesting that all around the state people organized prayer vigils and set up refreshments on the streets. People spoke nicely to one another. For the first time, I saw camaraderie in action as people were sharing what they had, helping one another, and empathizing with one another. New York busy life style slowed down, one no longer heard people honking out of impatience, and I could see passersby saying hello to others a rarity prior to the tragedy. The lesson of this, however, is that we all belong to one human family united by the creator of the universe. We are indispensable. What affects one person affects others. We ought to love one another, care for one another, and help one another no matter our race, ethnicity, religious beliefs, and socioeconomic status.

When tragedy occurs, it is very difficult to trust God. I was happy that people resorted to praying more amidst the tragedy. God really intervened and brought healing to the nation. This healing did not take place in a day, it was a gradual process. We know that trusting God and people takes time but immersing oneself in the word of God helps a great deal. This is because in the Word there is hope and encouragement. If you are experiencing loss right now, can you please trust God? Can you allow the love of God to work in you lifting, rebuilding, and equipping you? Friend, He will never leave nor forsake you (Hebrews: 13:5). Let this love, the love of God help you heal and cause you to grow. If you allow this, it will not only bring you freedom and growth but will also guarantee you victory. I ask you to choose the way of God, believe Him, accept Him and that peace that passes all understanding will overwhelm you and lead you to a glorious eternity. Indeed, as a community we overcame the losses of the September 11, 2001 by acknowledging and involving God. Can we continue to renew our faith in Him and trust Him to be with us in our everyday lives? Can we call on God now to be present in our lives rather than wait till we have another crisis? Can we invite Jesus into our hearts to become the center of our lives?

Years ago as a young person, I noticed that no matter how happy I was it ended up in sadness. I would be happy, bubbly, and having fun then all of a sudden the happiness would turn into sadness for no known reason at all. Some people might call it depression but I would call it the absence of Jesus in my life then. I went to church, participated in church doctrines, prayed to the saints, went to confessions, and took communions and yet sadness resided in me. However, when I became saved, born-again, that sadness was replaced by Jesus residing at the center of my heart. Once I allowed Jesus to take over my life He took residence and no matter what life brings He brightens my day. I pray that you ask Jesus to come into your life so that He can be at the center of your heart as He is in mine. I have the drawing of my pre-born again and born-again hearts as follows:

Pre-born again heart (old heart). Jesus
in a little spot in my heart.

Born-again heart (new heart). Jesus at
the center of my heart and life.

Children and Their
Understanding Regarding Death

My children love pets especially fish and dogs. I love pets too but I could not succumb to their clamor for a dog because I was not ready to care for one. I promised them that I would get them dogs when they grew older and able to care for them. We went and got gold fish instead. My son Uche named his pet fish Daniel and my daughter Ada named hers Genesis. Now, after a couple of days Genesis died and then Daniel followed suit. They were filled with sadness at this experience of loss and I assured them I would get them another, and I did. However, we buried the two fish in the backyard. I used that opportunity to teach them about death and burial. Boy, did they have lots of questions? You bet! They bombarded me with many, such as, "Is that how grandma and grandpa were buried when they died?" "Will they get up again?" Ada said to me, "I wish my grandma and grandpa did not die." She further said, "Mommy, I will get you a mother that will never die." I hugged, kissed, and thanked her for her thoughtfulness and care. I then explained to her the impossibility of such and she eventually understood. She and her brother always express that they wish they had grandpa and grandma, especially, when they see other kids with their grandparents. Sometimes when they are upset, they will cry to their grandparents, "grandma I need y-----o------u!!" "Grandpa, I need y---o---u!!!!" as if they can hear them. I really do feel sorry for them and wish their grandparents were alive. But the reality is that death had snatched them away before my children could see or know them. To make up, my husband and I tell them stories about these wonderful grandparents and that gives them some memories.

Nevertheless, so many of their fish died and we replaced them. One day we got two chickens. They were cute and my son Uche was scared of them. He would scream and run away if they came near him. Ada who encouraged me to get them was very excited at first but started losing interest the first few minutes we brought them home. She complained that they did poop and that she did not like the smell and that I should send them back. I talked to her and eventually her interest was renewed and she loved, played, and petted them. After a couple of days, she said, "mommy, maybe we should not be getting another fish, maybe we should get only chicks that do not die." And then, she added, "I don't like that the fish keep dying and dying." Ada was very right by what she said and how she felt. I told her that I wished there was no death. Don't we all wish the same? Though we replaced the fish but she was still not happy. In her little mind she still felt and understood the concept of death and loss.

Children will one way or another see, hear, or experience death or loss. It is up to adults to prepare them for it using any available tool or medium they can understand. For example, my son Uche, a third grader then, came home one day with an assignment to read which was about children who lost loved ones. I read it with him and his sister Ada and we also watched the video clips. They felt for and empathized with those children. The bottom line, however, is that death is inevitable and we should prepare for it and the love of God will always keep us strong. I have heard so many stories of parents dying while they were alone with their young children. Recently, a four year old stayed with his dead mother in the home for about four days till a friend stopped by and contacted the authorities. There have been many other children who had similar experiences, and most of them did not understand what was happening. We really need to start preparing and talking to our children about death. That will help prepare them when it happens. I was happy that my son's teacher gave the class such home work.

Uche and Ada with their fish pets (Arizona).

Neighbor's Pain Now My Pain

One day, we were getting ready for the night when my husband who was temporarily in New York called. During our conversation, he reported that his niece's one year old daughter was very sick and that he had just spoken with the family and after prayers advised them to take her to the hospital. I told him that the kids and I would join in prayers too. Shortly after, as I was brushing my teeth for the night, my daughter, Adaeze, four year old, ran to me with my cell phone in her hand saying, "Mommy, mommy see "Honey, baby died." I immediately turned and asked her what she was saying as she was handing the phone to me. It turned out to be a text message from my husband that stated "Honey, baby died." I immediately burst into tears and screamed so loud that my poor child was scared. My son Uche ran to us and both of them were sad and cried too. They also became afraid and my daughter said, "Mommy I don't like when babies die because I love them." I held her very tightly and told her that I didn't like it either. We later prayed and got ready to sleep with my daughter clinging to me and eventually slept. It took a fewer minutes before Uche slept too.

Early the next morning, however, as I was helping Uche get ready for school, I looked out of the window. Across the street were ambulances and police vehicles. People were driving in and parking their vehicles and going into the neighbor's house. Few minutes later a police ambulance came. People probably family members and friends with their children (babies, teens, and young adults) were trooping into the house crying and hugging one another. Then I thought to myself how thousands of miles away in Nigeria my in-laws were mourning the death of the little baby and here in my neighborhood in the United States another family is mourning the loss of someone. What a world full of tragedy. My neighbor's pain became my pain. I felt so sorry for them. I wished I could go there immediately to console them. As I couldn't do much at that point I prayed for them. Eventually, canopies were set up outside the house. Garage door was opened and turned into a gathering space. People began going in and out bringing sleeping bags, chairs, and anything that would make them comfortable as they mourned. Also cars drove in and out and the street became overcrowded with vehicles of different colors, makes, and models. Someone had been lost and would never be seen again forever! What a painful experience.

A couple of hours later, I decided to go there and commiserate with them even though I did not know them. People were sitting; some standing; and they were all talking in low voices. I waved to the crowd beckoning on one to come. A woman filled with sadness on her face came over to me. I introduced myself to her as a neighbor and told her that I observed the ambulance and people crying and wanted to know if everything was okay and if I could help in any way. She started crying. We hugged and I consoled her. She told me that her twenty seven year old daughter passed away that morning. She went on to say that her daughter was diagnosed with cancer a month prior. She lived in the house with her husband and two kids the younger being only four years old. She said that she appreciated my stopping by. I told her that I had been praying for them since I observed the incident and asked her if she believed in God. She passionately said, "yes I do." She told me that her deceased daughter started going to a Christian church with her entire family recently. I told her that I would continue to pray for them and that God would see them through. I also told her that I might have seen her daughter because each time we passed by the house we usually saw kids and adults playing outside and that they were really friendly. I asked her if there was anything they needed so that I could go get it for them. She said that they were okay and did not need anything. I told her that I had some folding chairs that I could lend to them and she gladly accepted to have them. I and my daughter who was with me went back to the house and brought the chairs to them. She was very appreciative. As the days went by I saw fewer visitors to the place until the immediate family was all alone with memory of their loved one being the only thing that they held onto with the agonizing and painful reality to live each day without her.

Meanwhile, I had spoken with my distraught niece-in-law who was on the other side of the world, in faraway Africa going through her own loss. I consoled and encouraged her. I told her how she had been a tower of strength and an encouragement to many. This young lady has suffered so much pain. Her husband was murdered about a year prior while she was pregnant leaving her with a three year old daughter who will never cease to ask "where is Daddy?" and all of a sudden she faced the loss of the second daughter who never even saw her father. What a life!

You know, when death or loss occurs, it affects the entire family; children, adults, neighbors, and even passersby. The reality is that we cannot run away from it. We cannot stop it from affecting our younger generations either. The truth is that even if young children have not experienced death or any kind of loss they will come across it somehow or somewhere; in school, story times, with friends, etc. They have to be taught how to deal with the emotions involved.

There are so many emotional issues involved in losing someone, such as denial, regrets, anger, bitterness, and others with devastating consequences. However, regret is one of the difficult ones. One expresses regret over many things: It could be something like not forgiving or reconciling with the person before he or she died; it could be not being able to do something for the person while he or she was alive, etc. That is why we should not procrastinate in settling issues with people for one never knows what may happen next. We should also heed the advice of Romans 12:18, "If it be possible, as much as lieth in you, live peaceably with all men"(KJV). Regret has negative consequences such as people committing suicide because they could not take it anymore. Sometimes, it leads to serious depression and other psychological problems. Someone I know faced the trauma of regret after she lost her seven year old son through auto accident. This child loved his mother so much and yearned for her to spend more time with him and take him to the park but got excuses in return. She always told him that she had no time. Unfortunately, when this child died unexpectedly, this lady was devastated. She regretted not having the time to spend with her son. She became so depressed that she started hearing voices of her son telling her to go to the park with him. Sometimes she would go to the park and sorrowfully cried out for her son to join her. It was too late for anything to be done as opportunities lost are always irretrievable. She now takes consolation in the fact that she will see him one day to part no more. She also enjoys reading the bible which has provided her with God's promises and peace. When we find ourselves in this kind of situation we should try and forgive ourselves and ask God to forgive us too. Also the bible should be our companion as we read and meditate on the Word as much as possible. Doing this builds our faith and brings encouragement.

The Dream: Christmas Gift and the Map

In December of 2012, I began feeling the urge to move out of New York City. It was surprising to my husband who had been suggesting for years that we move to a warmer climate. He was very happy. We began praying and seeking the Lord's direction as well as going online researching states as the bible says, faith without work is dead (James 2:14). One fateful day, as I was praying around 5 am regarding where we should move to, the Holy Spirit asked me if I remember the dream I had many years before my son was born. My mind immediately went to the dream I had over ten years ago about "The Map" which comprised two episodes. In my first dream the scene was around Christmas time. I was given a Christmas gift wrapped in a cloth. The gift was in form of a baby. I joyfully carried it from the parking lot in both arms into my new house. The picture is still very clear in my memory. In the Second dream, the scene was like in a community with beautiful houses, trees, and flowers. I was given a map. I looked at it and didn't know what to do with it. Still in that dream I asked a bishop friend of ours who was visiting what I should do with the map. He told me that maybe God wanted me to go there and do evangelism and the dream ended. Immediately I woke up and quickly picked up a piece of paper and drew the map. It looked somehow similar to either the map of the state I was born or the island where I was residing at that time but not exactly. For many days I wondered exactly what to make of this dream or what I should do with this map, and I was not sure. Should I go back to Africa and stay there and evangelize? Should I stay on the island and do same? I prayed and asked God to lead me to exactly what he wanted me to do with the map. I remember telling a pastor friend who came from the same country with me about it and my consideration to go back to Africa and he wondered why I should do that when God had already brought me to the promised land of America. I told him that I was ready to go to wherever the lord sent me. Nevertheless, I began planning to move back to Africa but later the plan was not successful.

Many years after these very significant dreams my husband joined me in the USA, and the following year our son, Martin-Richard Uchechukwu (named after my husband, dad, and sister) was born. Four and half years after, my daughter, Christa Adaeze was also born. However, when my son was born an amazing thing happened. The same map that was given to me in my dream was on his back as a birth mark! Wonders shall never cease! When I asked the doctor what the mark was she said it was "Mongolian Spot" (birthmark). According to the doctor, such marks may be associated with medical problems. She suggested that it had to be examined to ascertain what it was. They did and no problem was found. Though it was believed to be a medical issue I was seeing something spiritual instead.

Nevertheless, it was amazing that on that day while I was praying for a place for us to relocate to the Holy Spirit reminded me of this map. I quickly rushed to Uche (as we fondly call him) while he was fast asleep, turned, examined, and took picture of the map on his back and began comparing it with different maps in the United States. Low and behold, it was a map in Arizona! I screamed, and screamed, tears of joy dripping down my cheek. I immediately called my husband who was far away at work that night. He was working night shift in addition to pastoring a church. I excitedly said to him, "Honey, God has answered our prayers; we are moving to Arizona; God is great and never fails." I related the above story to him. He was excited too. He could not wait to get home early in the morning to compare the maps himself. When he got home I couldn't even wait for him to take a shower and he couldn't wait either. He compared the maps himself and was amazed. We began praising God. What a faithful God we serve. The God that answers prayers! The God that is able to do exceeding abundantly above all that we ask or think… (Ephesians 3:20). From that moment we began getting ready to move to Arizona. We told the kids. They were excited but complained that they would miss their friends and extended relatives. I agreed with them and told them I felt the same but that we would keep in touch with them. However, anywhere we saw the map of Arizona we stood and took pictures with it.

Map of USA with Ada standing on Arizona (New York).

I contacted my friend Jessica who had lived in New York as well as Arizona. She said she loved Arizona and frankly testified that it was the best place that she had ever lived. My husband and I earnestly and extensively made reviews of the state online, sometimes using Google Earth. It was amazing and very beautiful. We could not wait to move. My husband was excited about the mountains but that was a drawback for me since I had little nervousness about them.

However, we decided that I go "spy out" the land before we could be sure that we would move. Miraculously we got in contact with family friends of ours, Donald and Yvette, whom we never knew had moved to Arizona. We made arrangements with them and I visited. It was a glorious visit. I fell in love with the place. Bro. Don and Sister Yvette as we fondly call them were the best hosts ever! They made me comfortable in their beautiful home and drove me around and showed me the city. While in their home I excitedly spoke with my sister Norah in Nigeria. I told her that I was in Arizona which is about three days driving or four to five hours of flight from New York City. I also told her that Arizona was my "Canaan land." She was happy for me and we prayed and asked God for more direction, guidance, and protection. That night, since I couldn't go back to sleep because of the time difference (NY being ahead of AZ by 3 hours), I decided to do what I love doing: putting my thoughts in writing. So I wrote:

ARIZONA, MY CANAAN LAND
This is my Canaan Land
    The Promised Land
        The Land of fulfillment
            The Land of peace
            The Land of joy
                The Land of hope
                    The Land of Beauty
                        The Land of God.

I praise you oh Lord for your infinite goodness
I praise you Lord for your righteousness and your awesomeness
I praise you Lord for your mercy

    and joy
      and peace
        and hope
          and strength
            and direction
              and guidance
                and most of all for being my God.

I praise you oh Lord!

Father Lord I praise your holy name for you have preserved me till this day
Lord I praise you for bringing me into the Land of abundance
Lord I praise you for your people who have opened their home and hearts to me
Lord I praise you that you have blessed them and they will remain blessed forever
Lord I praise you for answered prayers
Father I praise you for your favors.

Lord we cried out to you and you answered
For your names' sake, we have not cherished sin in our hearts and so Lord, you have listened
    Thank you for guiding and protecting us
      Thank you for not rejecting our prayers

Thank you for not withholding your love from us

Thank you Lord for everything.

After this visit we made up our minds to move but I struggled with the right time to tender my resignation letter. However, about two weeks before I was to do it, a meeting of all directors at my agency was called at the headquarters in New York City. During the meeting we were informed that the agency was downsizing. I was among the program directors that were being laid off. I was excited and overjoyed. I did not wait to get home to tell my husband. I called him immediately and gave him the good news which otherwise would have been a bad one. He too was elated. God will always turn bad news to good news for His children. Being laid off meant that I would be compensated financially and also entitled to unemployment benefits. I saw it as a way of my God saying, "my daughter be equipped for your move to your promised land." What a mighty God we serve! This is the God that delights in the prosperity of His servants; the God that supplies our need according to His riches in glory by Christ Jesus. If I had submitted my resignation letter earlier I would not have gotten any severance check or unemployment package. The on time God, the God who knows the end from the beginning, the God who is never late did it for me!

The Tempest

As we were basking in the euphoria of the financial miracle associated with my job loss and the decision to relocate the enemy of our souls was fiercely upset. Just like the Israelites, we encountered lots of setbacks. Also, just like Jesus and His disciples the enemy raised a tempest against us. It was terrible how the defeated roaring lion fought against our journey to the Promised Land. One night an unknown person dumped garbage in front of our house. When my husband came back from work early in the morning he wanted to take it out but decided to do it later as he was very tired. When I got up I decided to do some cleaning outside our house. Taking the dumped garbage to put in a trash can by the corner of the house I suddenly slipped and completely broke my left wrist. I was in so much pain and agony. I screamed "please call 911, call 911." My husband heard me and quickly sprang out of bed, ran downstairs, and helped me up and called 911. I found myself in the hospital where the fight to save my wrist began. It took months before I got healed by God's grace. Though this injury delayed our journey for some months we kept strong and never wavered. We knew that the devil was fighting us because of what God had planned for us in Arizona. I recall telling my doctor about the relocation and she said that maybe God did not want us to relocate. I told her that I had no doubt that God wanted us to go and that it was the devil trying to stop us because he knew what God had kept in store for us in Arizona. She smiled and said that it could be true too.

However, it was during this time that my husband and I organized a free giveaway of tons of foods, clothing, and other materials to over two hundred families in Staten Island through ALL Power Heritage Ministries Inc. (a ministry we founded) to the glory of Almighty God. I was able to type all the flyers and other materials used for the occasion with only one hand as the other was on cast and God was glorified. Again the enemy was shamed as the delay to relocate led to the name of God Almighty being lifted up.

I, Frances with broken wrist assisting with the
free giveaway. The devil failed (New York).

When the time came, God in His infinite goodness made the relocation smooth and successful. God provided all the support we needed for the journey both financially and emotionally. It was great knowing that God was in support of our move. What shall we then say to these things? If God be for us, who can be against us? (Romans 8:31). Nevertheless, it was about six months after my job ended that we made it to our "Promised Land." Arizona is truly a very beautiful land surrounded by wonderful mountains, with the landscape boasting of beautiful trees of all kinds, flowers, animals, edible and none edible fruits and nuts. It reminds me of some places and stories in the bible, such as Moses going to the mountains and others we see in Christian movies.

One morning, as I dropped my son off to school, and driving home, I was overwhelmed with emotions how wonderful it is to live in such natural beauty. Our neighborhood is so beautifully adorned with modern houses, trees, flowers, and tranquility that one cares less about the high temperatures which I love anyway. After all, it occurs only in the months of summer. How lucky I am to experience such beautiful scenery and climate. I call it the land of A Z, the land with the beginning alphabet A and ending alphabet Z (the land of the beginning and the end). God is doing wonderful things in our lives here already. Devil, the egregious liar has lost the battle.

Is God Real?

Is God Real?

Many people by reason of struggles and other events in their lives have questioned the reality of God. I for sure did so too. I believe that many people who profess atheism do so because of one life's disappointment or the other. Let's face it, how can one explain why good people die early as I earlier discussed in this book? How can a lady whose pastor husband was murdered in cold blood only to have death snatch her baby not be tempted to question God's reality? How can a loving God watch His children ravaged and killed by diseases, auto accidents, plane crashes, terrorism, and other evil forces and He stands aloof? Nevertheless, if we juxtapose what He "failed" to do and what He has done we discover that the latter is greater. In the first place, we don't even need to make comparison what He did or did not do because He says He is the Alpha and the Omega, the beginning and the end (Revelation 22:13). By the way, did God really fail to do those things or did He allow them to happen for a reason? God has proved in my life that He is real. When I remember His miracles despite all the losses, both human and material, I have reasons to bless His Holy Name. His mercies towards me are endless. As the popular Christian song goes,

"Count your blessings,
name them one by one,
Count your blessings,
See what God hath done! ...."

What about you? What do you remember He has done for you? Can you write down God's miracles in your life? Can you name them? Can you share them with people? If you do you will see how your faith will balloon. Do you know that God's testimonies in your life are powerful weapons to fight the devil and his lies which bring doubt, worry, fear, and depression? Revelation 12:11 says, "And they overcame him by the blood of the Lamb and by the word of their testimony..." (KJV). I am sharing all these testimonies to counteract the devils attacks against you and me. I am also doing this to help build your faith because faith comes by hearing, and hearing by the word of God (Romans 10:17 NKJV).

LETTER TO GOD AND THE MIRACLOUS ANSWER

A couple of years ago, shortly after my graduation at the New York University I decided to write a letter to God. Yeah, amazing right? How can one write a letter to God when He is invisible? How will you mail it to Him? Well, I did write the letter. God is invisible and omnipresent too. I wrote this letter and put it in one of the walk-in closets I converted into my prayer room. In the letter I reminded God of His promise of being the father to the fatherless and how He promised to supply all our need according to His riches in glory by Christ Jesus. I told Him that I had accrued student loans that needed to be paid off and as His daughter He needed to help me pay. God miraculously provided the money that covered the student loan worth over $80,000 through the sale of my house. I recall my neighbor saying to me, "You must have connection upstairs," meaning connection with God. I cheerfully agreed that I did. Are you in debt? Are you facing eviction because you owe rent or mortgage? Are you struggling to make payment on that house or car? Are credit card debts and payments depriving you of comfort and joy? Please call upon Him. He says to call upon Him in the day of trouble and He will deliver you (Psalm 50: 15). God's love never fails (Psalm 136:1).

I Can Do All Things Through Christ Who Strengthens Me

I have come to a point in my life that I can declare without any fear of contradiction that nothing is too difficult for the lord. I have also seen the enormity of His unflinching faithfulness which gives me the motivation to declare that He is real and never fails and that I can do all things by His help! When I sold my first house the proceeds of which the Lord used to help me pay my student loan, and moved into the new one which I bought thereafter, I decided to complete the attic. The men who were remodeling the rooms neglected to follow the instruction I gave them to carve out storage places. When I found this out and insisted they do something about it they explained that they had already finished the walls. When they left that evening I went on my knees and prayed to God for wisdom and strength and quickly sprang into action. He answered and gave me an extraordinary strength that I used to cut open two of the walls with some tools. When the men came the following morning they were astonished and could not believe their eyes. They asked me how I was able to do it. I told them, "I can do all things through Christ who strengthens me" (Phil. 4: 13). Sometimes we limit ourselves by dwelling on sight and not by faith. We ought to always work by faith and not by sight (2 Corinthians 5:7).

I, Frances cutting the walls in the attic. I can do all things through Christ who strengthens me (New York).

The universe is full of endless and limitless opportunities we can harness to the glory of God. We can be greater than we are if we can de-emphasize fear and strongly believe that we can do anything by the anointing God has given us. Friend, you can start that new business. You can start that ministry. You can go back to school and acquire more education no matter how young or old you are. You can resolve that marriage dispute or faltering relationship with your child, family member(s), friends, and others. You can get that husband or wife or child. These can be possible if you believe. He is the God that answers by fire. I remember a story my husband told me about what happened to him when he was in high school. A few weeks before his final exams he lost all his text books and notes. He was distraught and scared. After thinking about what to do he quickly rushed to his elder brother for money to replace the books. His brother gave him the money but added that though it seemed almost too late to read all that was required to prepare for the exams that he should believe that he would make it. He explained that he believed and trusted God and came out with flying colors. The enemy can bring obstacles on our way, disappointment and frustration can overwhelm us, the journey can appear too long and tortuous, and problems can seem insurmountable but if we believe and trust the Lord of the universe we can make it. This is why Jesus declared in Mark 9:23, "…If thou canst believe, all things are possible to him that believeth" (KJV).

The Cry: Jesus H-E-L-P M-E!

After the purchase of that second house in New York, one day I got a mail from the City that they planned to redo my sidewalk and stated the amount I should pay that ran into thousands of dollars. I was concerned because the amount was too much for me to cough out at that time. I thought about what to do. I also wondered if private contractors would be cheaper. I didn't know who to turn to for advice as I was living alone at the time. I went into my room and started crying out to God. I remember crying "J-e-s-u-s please help m--e; help me, Jesus help me." I believe I cried so loud that people on the street might have heard me. As I was crying out to God I heard a voice tell me to go to the window and look. I immediately went and looked. It was surprising who I saw - the former owner of the house; the right person I needed to talk to about the letter. Meanwhile, I had been trying to reach her and could not find her contact information. I immediately ran downstairs and hurried to meet her at the side entrance to the first floor of the house. However, she appeared sad and tears flooded her eyes. I embraced her and told her that I was happy to see her and asked her if she was okay. She told me that she was leaving the city and needed to come to the house to say goodbye to it for the last time. She asked me if it was okay for her to go inside. Luckily, I had not rented it out so I obliged her and she was very thankful. She sorrowfully went in and said her goodbye to the empty apartment downstairs while I waited outside. She told me that she and her husband had lived there all their lives and had no children. She had to rent out the second floor when her husband passed away to have companions. She said that all her life memories were in that house. I felt so sorry for her. I gave her some words of encouragement and shared my own stories about life's vicissitudes with her. I also told her about the letter I received from the City regarding their plan to fix the sidewalk. She said to me, "you are the luckiest person to get that letter." She said that she waited for it from the City for years and never got it! She told me that it was cheaper for them to do it than private contractors. Later I checked and found out that she was right. Another amazing and miraculous part of this story was that during the sale of the house a certain amount was deducted for the fixing of the side walk and I did not remember or realize it. I found out that it would only take half of that amount to pay the City for doing it! God is awesome. He sees and plans ahead for His children. His miracles come when they are highly needed so that His name will be glorified. In the very nick of time God brought the former owner to calm me down and save me from unnecessary anguish. The Lord will also do it for you when you cry out to him. Amen.

High Blood Pressure, God's Intervention

A few months after moving to Arizona, I began having weird feelings. My body was just telling me that something was wrong. After being medically evaluated it was found that my blood pressure (BP) was high. I wondered what might be the reason - high sodium which I noticed in the water? Genetics? Lack of exercise? What could it be? My Primary Care Physician (PCP) decided that she would not diagnose me with having high blood pressure immediately. She advised me to monitor it for about four weeks and come back to her with my results. She also advised that I walk at least 20 minutes each day, cut down on my salt and food intake, monitor and record my BP. Though I had done these before I had the symptom I decided to cut even more. Nevertheless, I began praying to God to please prevent this high blood pressure.

On the fourth week before going back to my PCP, that morning I prayed and trusted God that it would be normal but it was still high after the doctor checked it.

I felt very sad. However, she suggested I start taking medication. I just could not imagine myself on such daily regimen. I asked her if there was an alternative and she suggested I try watching my diet and lose some weight. She gave me another one month to come back. I vehemently refused to allow fear overwhelm me and began trusting God. I believed that God would heal me, and He did. My blood pressure became normal and I also lost some weight. When I went back to my PCP after one month she was shocked and very happy for me. Till date my blood pressure has been normal. When I look back I see the hand of God in it. If not for the fact that I trusted Him I would have accepted the problem and would have begun the medication regimen fearing that without it I might develop a more serious ailment. "Trust in the LORD with all your heart and lean not on your own understanding; in all your ways submit to him, and he will make your paths straight" (Proverbs 3:5-6 (NIV).

It is wonderful to have faith in God because He will see you through. Trust the Lord with all your heart because His mercy endures forever (Psalm 136:1). Is your blood pressure high? Are you experiencing any type of illness? Trust God and He will heal you. Remember His words "...for I am the LORD, who heals you" (Exodus 15:26 (NIV). He also says that if you call upon Him in the day of trouble, He will deliver you (Psalm 50:15). Cast all your cares upon God because He cares for you (1Peter 5:7). Be careful for nothing; but in everything, by prayer and supplication with thanksgiving let your requests be made known unto God (Philippians 4: 6). As you can see I am a living testimony of God's healing mercies. Trust God and do not waver. Also remember that the enemy of our souls, the devil, does not give up. That is why the bible warns us to "be sober, be vigilant; because your adversary the devil walks about like a roaring lion, seeking whom he may devour" (1 Peter 5:8 (NKJV).

The Miraculous Shortened Trip

Something unbelievable happened during those trying periods when I was in New York City. It was after getting the news that my other uncle had passed away leaving his wife and six young children. I was extremely very sad and weakened by the news. I didn't feel like going to work that morning as I was very grief stricken but remembering the fact that my then supervisor had questioned my reports of incessant deaths in my family and had told me that I was lying and making them up I managed to get up. As I was getting ready I looked at the clock and it was 8 am. Meanwhile, I was supposed to be at work by 9 am. It usually took about two hours to my job and my trip involved taking the public bus to the Ferry terminal, taking the ferry to cross over to Manhattan, and then catching the train to my office. The possibility of getting to work on time that day was ruled out. I cried out to God and begged Him to miraculously cause me to get to work at 9 am. By human standard it was impossible to achieve that feat. Having prayed, I quickly got ready as fast as I could and left. On my way, I refused to look at the watch because I did not want to aggravate myself. As soon as I got to work, I looked at my watch, it was 9 am. I could not believe it. God miraculously shortened my trip. Till this day, I do not know how He did it but I know that He is the God that is able to do all things. Our God will do the same for you. Whenever you feel that you cannot do it or achieve your goals call upon the Lord and He will help you. Isaiah 41:19, "Fear thou not; for I am with thee: be not dismayed; for I am thy God: I will strengthen thee; yea, I will help thee; yea, I will uphold thee with the right hand of my righteousness" (KJV).

God's Appointment for Me With A Stranger

During my first few years here in the United States I was heading to work one morning and as I was getting into my car I spotted a man in his 60s who seemed unconscious lying on the parking lot. I rushed to him and asked him if he was okay. He mumbled something. I was not sure what was happening to him and he did not seem to be drunk. I knew I had to act fast. I looked around to see if someone was around to assist by calling 911 (emergency) while I stay by him and encourage him but there was no one. I rushed back to my car, put my pocket book down, and immediately called 911 while glancing at him. As soon as I finished speaking with the dispatcher who assured me that the ambulance was on the way I went over to him and told him that help was on the way and began talking to him about the love of Jesus. I told him that Jesus loved him and I prayed over him and asked him to pray the sinner's prayer with me. He mumbled after me. As soon as we finished the prayer the police and the ambulance came and took him away.

I heaved a sigh of relief, thanked God, and headed to work.

One day after locating where he lived I went to his apartment and knocked on the door with the hope of seeing him. Someone came out and informed me that he had passed away. I was sad but thankful to God for giving him the opportunity to hear about Jesus and possibly saved. His family members did not know what transpired between him and his God before his passing. God is awesome and performs His miracles any time.

Friend, if you have family members that passed away and you doubt if they made it to heaven be consoled for you never know if someone might have helped them get saved or they might have confessed Him on their own. Remember the story of my late atheist uncle. Indeed, it is very important for everyone to be prepared for the D-day by accepting Jesus as Lord and Savior and to keep praying for loved ones as God may use you or any other person to bring them to Himself.

All To My Advantage

When Jesus was on earth satan fought very hard to frustrate His ministry by instigating the people to crucify him. I could picture the devil and his minions celebrating as the multitude shouted "crucify him, crucify him." The son of perdition rejoiced as our Savior was cruelly nailed to the cross. What the devil did not know, however, was that His crucifixion and death would lead to the salvation of mankind. Likewise the death of my parents and other loved ones. The enemy thought that their loss would break me. It made me stronger instead. Most importantly, they made it to heaven. Sometimes I wonder what would have happened if they did not go to be with the Lord when they did. I, however, leave it to the Lord who is the author and finisher of our faith, the decider of our destiny. Moreover, I know that as long as the Lord is concerned all things work together for good to them that love God, to them who are the called according to his purpose (Romans 8:28). God has a way of turning what the enemy thinks is evil against us to our advantage, and that is why I say, all to my advantage! Child of God rejoice, fear not, worry not, and fret not for we have a God who absolutely delights in our prosperity.

It is amazing that I am writing and talking about death in this book. As already stated, death is something I feared a lot as a child. Growing up, if I heard of any one dying whether it was a relative or a stranger for days I would not eat. I would mourn, and mourn, and mourn. Now I am stronger because of Jesus who has transformed my life and given me extraordinary courage. Now I know that death may happen at any point in our lives or in the lives of our loved ones and that we may not be able to stop it. However, my consolation, courage, and strength to deal with the myriad of deaths around me came from the sword of the spirit which is the word of God. That is the reason I wrote this poem about the Bible, thus:

MY BIBLE, MY OASIS
My Bible, my Oasis
My treasure in my desert world
My vegetation in my desert land
My spring and water source
My book and energy source
My food, my drink
My companion and my Peace
My caravan that takes me to the world beyond
My Bible, my Oasis.

The Bible, my Oasis
The story of love

The love of a father to his children
The story of the one that lays down His life
The story of love of man laying down his life for another
The story of Jesus, the Lamb who laid down his life
for us all
The love of God to us all
The greater love, from the God of all
The Bible, my Oasis.

The Bible, my Oasis
The story of sinners
The story of the one that wiped away our sins
The story of "while we were yet sinners, Jesus Christ
died for us all"
The story of the how of the wicked
The story of the redemption from the wicked
The story of the inevitability of death
The story of the strong enemy of man
The story of the death conqueror, Jesus
The Bible, my Oasis.

Reflection

This book was written with tears. Every memory of my loved ones still brings tears. Sometimes tears of joy that Dad, Mom, sister, other relatives- uncles, aunts-in-law, sister-in-law, father-in-law, and mother-in-law may have made it to heaven, and sometimes tears of regret that I did not do all the things I wanted to do for them or get all the information that I wanted to get from them or the fact that my children didn't have the opportunity to see their loving grandparents and other extended family members. Also, I have tears that not all of them may have made it to heaven. Life is fragile and unpredictable. That is why it is very important that we celebrate family because a living person now may be a dead person in the next minute. Most importantly, it is very necessary that we all have a personal relationship with our Lord Jesus, knowing that He is the savior of our souls. When that happens, we know for sure that whether we live or die we belong to Christ. However, during the time of mourning my Dad, I was afraid I was developing hypergraphia (obsessive writing). I was writing down all my thoughts in my dairies which

I always kept from childhood, on post-it, pieces of papers, and other materials and pasting them all around the house, in the kitchen, bathrooms, hallways, and other places. I wrote scriptures and encouraging words that stated that I would be okay. I wrote things like… "Dad went to be with the Lord." "I will see him again in heaven." "I will meet him to part no more." "I am a child of God and He will never leave nor forsake me." "I am strong." "I am a conqueror." "I am the daughter of the Most High God." "I can do all things through Christ who strengthens me," etc. I was constantly reminded by those words that I needed to live and defeat the devil. It is amazing that some of them became relevant for this book. God is good and leads us to do things that may be useful to us in future. He is the God of miracles.

PLEASE USE THE SPACE BELOW TO WRITE
DOWN ALL THE MIRACLES GOD HAS DONE IN
YOUR LIFE AND SHARE THEM WITH OTHERS. I
WILL ALSO BE GLAD IF YOU CAN SHARE THEM
WITH ME AT goodluckf@hotmail.com. YOU WILL
BE BLESSED AS YOU DO THIS AND THE NAME
OF GOD WILL BE GLORIFIED.

**LORD, I THANK YOU FOR ALL THESE
MIRACLES IN MY LIFE:**

_____

_____

_____

_____

_____

_____

_____

_____

_____

_____

_____

_____

_____

_____

_____

_____

_____

_____

PATIENTLY WAIT ON THE LORD:

Dear Friend, if your miracle has not come yet please patiently wait on the Lord and keep trusting. He will renew your strength and will cause his love to shine upon you. He will give you your heart's desire in due season. Also while you wait please pray without ceasing. As I waited on the Lord for some answers to my prayers, especially before my husband joined me here in the United States, what I did was pray in the manner in which I wrote the poem below:

WHILE AWAITING HIM!

Lord while I await your miracles,
may I love you more.
As I wait on you,
may I learn to do your will.
As I wait for the answers to my prayers,
may I seek your face and know what your plan is for my life.

As I wait for my husband,
may I pray for other marriages.
As I wait for my own children,
may I love and help other people's children.
As I wait for my house,
may I pray for other people's houses and homes.

As I wait on you Lord,
I trust that the Angels will hover around me.
As I wait on you,

I trust that you will keep me safe.
As I wait on you Lord,
I trust that your Holy Spirit will minister to me day and night.

As I wait on you Lord,
May peace and calm pervade me.
As I wait on you,
may I continue to seek your face and pray without ceasing.
As I wait on you,
may I never be distracted by things of the world.

As I wait on you,
may no friend or acquaintance lead me astray.
As I wait on you,
may I never leave your holy presence.
As I wait on you,
may I never cease to meditate on your awesomeness.

Sincere Love

For God so loved the world, that he gave his only begotten Son, that whosoever believeth in him should not perish, but have everlasting life (John 3:16). My dear friend, you are not reading this book by chance. You have the opportunity now to get it right with God. If you already have, thank God. If not please try for the benefit are tremendous. What about your friends and relatives? Can you please share the good news of Jesus with them? You can also get a copy of this book for them for you will be glad you did. God is ever ready to step in and help us with whatever is troubling us as you have read through the testimonies shared in this book. He says to come to Him all we that labor and are heavy laden that He will give us rest: rest from sin, fear, worry, anxiety, depression, and whatever it is that bothers us. Most importantly, He gives us eternal life. The bible teaches us that whether we live or die, we belong to God. My Cri de Coeur is that you accept Jesus as your lord and personal savior. Please note that the salvific truth is that Jesus Christ came for us all.

SALVATION PRAYER

"Dear Jesus, I am a sinner. I come to you now. I am sorry for my sins. I ask you to please forgive me and come into my life. I make you my Lord and personal Savior. I belong to you now. I decree and declare that I am born again in the name of Jesus. Amen."

If you pray the above prayer with all your heart, just believe that the Lord has forgiven you and that you are now born again. It is as simple as that. Continue to trust Him to finish the work He has begun in you. You can find fellowship in a Christ centered or believing Church near you. Please pass this on to family members, friends, and other loved ones. May the Lord keep you and bless you. May his love shine upon you. Amen.

For the saved I know that sometimes it is not easy for the people in our lives to really understand the reality of God so we have to keep praying for them and trusting God to bring them to Himself. Please use the space below to write down the names of relatives, friends, and others you are trusting God to save. Keep praying and trusting and He will deliver them. Also see a sample of prayer for your loved ones below.

LORD I PRAY FOR THE FOLLOWING:

_____

_____

_____

_____

_____

_____

_____

_____

_____

_____

_____

_____

_____

_____

_____

_____

_____

_____

_____

_____

_____

_____

_____

_____

_____

_____

_____

PRAYER FOR LOVED ONES

"Dear Lord, I surrender my loved ones to you. I ask you to please forgive them, and may they never leave this planet without making you their Lord and personal Savior. Please Lord meet them at the point of their needs and may your love shine upon them in the name of Jesus. Amen.

Some Famous People And Their Dying Words:

Jesus Christ as he hung on the cross: "Father, into thy hands I commend my spirit." *Luke 23:46*

***Stephen** (First Christian Martyr) as he was being stoned: "Lord Jesus, receive my spirit!"*

Richard Ebisike "I know I am qualified to be in heaven." And as he lay peacefully on his bed: "I have something to tell you......"

Andrew Jackson, US President: "Oh, do not cry - be good children and we will all meet in heaven."

Louis XIV, King of France: "Why do you weep? Did you think I was immortal?"

Leonardo da Vinci, artist: "I have offended God and mankind because my work did not reach the quality it should have."

Henry the Eight: "So, now all is gone- empire, Body and Soul!"

George Washington, US President: "I die hard but am not afraid to go."

Thomas Edison, American Inventor: "It's beautiful over there."

John Newton, Former Slave trader who later freed his slaves and advocated for freedom of slaves; the author of the song Amazing Grace, how sweet thy sound..: "I am still in the land of the dying; I shall be in the land of the living soon."

Dying Words of Atheists:

Caesar Borgia: "While I lived, I provided for everything but death; now I must die, and am unprepared to die."

Thomas Hobbs (a political philosopher) "I say again, if I had the whole world at my disposal, I would give it to live one day. I am about to take a leap into the dark."

Thomas Payne the leading atheistic writer in American colonies: "Stay with me for God's sake; I cannot bear to be left alone, O Lord help me! O God, what have I done to suffer so much? What will become of me hereafter? "I would give worlds if I had them, that The Age of Reason had never been published. O Lord, help me! Christ, help me! ...No, don't leave; stay with me! Send even a child to stay with me; for I am on the edge of Hell here alone. If ever the Devil had an agent, I have been that one."

Sir Thomas Scott, Chancellor of England "Until this moment I thought there was neither a God nor hell. Now

I know and feel that there are both, and I am doomed to perdition by the just judgment of the Almighty."

Voltaire (famous anti-Christian atheist): 'I am abandoned by God and man: I will give you half of what I am worth if you give me six month's life." (He said this to Dr. Fochin, who told him it could not be done). "Then shall I die and go to hell!" His nurse said: "For all the money in Europe I wouldn't want to see another unbeliever die! All night long he cried for forgiveness."

Hume David, atheist philosopher famous for his philosophy of empiricism and skepticism of religion, he cried loud on his death bed "I am in flames!" It is said "his desperation was a horrible scene."

Napoleon Bonaparte, the French emperor, and who, like Adolf Hitler brought death to millions to satisfy his greedy, power-mad selfish ambitions for world conquest: "I die before my time, and my body will be given back to the earth. Such is the fate of him who has been called the great Napoleon. What an abyss between my deep misery and the eternal kingdom of Christ!"

Sir Francis Newport, the head of an English Atheist club to those gathered around his deathbed: "You need not tell me there is no God for I know there is one, and that I am in His presence! You need not tell me there is no hell. I feel myself already slipping. Wretches, cease your idle talk about there being hope for me! I know I am lost forever! Oh, that fire! Oh the insufferable pangs of hell! …Oh, that I could lie for a thousand years upon the fire that is never quenched, to purchase the favor of God and be united with Him again. But it is a fruitless wish. Millions and millions of years will bring me no nearer to the end of my torments than one poor hour. Oh, eternity forever and forever! Oh, the insufferable pangs of Hell!"

Charles IX was the French who urged on by his mother, gave the order for the massacre of the French Huguenots, in which 15,000 souls were slaughtered in Paris alone and 100,000 in other sections of France, for no other reason than that they loved Christ. The guilty king suffered miserably for years after the event. He finally died, bathed in blood bursting from his veins. To his physicians he said in his last hours: "Asleep or awake, I see the mangled forms of the Huguenots passing before me. They drop with blood. They point at their open wounds. Oh, that I had spared at least the little infants at the bosom! What blood! I know not where I am. How will all this end? What shall I do? I am lost forever! I know it. Oh, I have done wrong."

David Straus, leading representative of German rationalism, after spending a lifetime erasing belief in God from the minds of others: "My philosophy leaves me utterly forlorn! I feel like one caught in the merciless jaws of an automatic machine, not knowing at what time one of its great hammers may crush me!"

In a Newsweek interview with Svetlana Stalin, the daughter of Joseph Stalin, she told of her father's death: "My father died a difficult and terrible death..God grant an easy death only to the just..At what seemed the very last moment he suddenly opened his eyes and cast a glance over everyone in the room. It was a terrible glance, insane or perhaps angry.. His left hand was raised, as though he were pointing to someone above and bringing down a curse on us all. The gesture was full of menace.. The next moment he was dead."

Anton LeVey author of the Satanic Bible and high priest of the religion dedicated to the worship of Satan. Some of his famous quotes are "There is a beast in man that needs to be exercised, not exorcised." His dying words were "Oh my, oh my, what have I done, there is something very wrong...there is something very wrong...."

Definition for the Young Minds:

Abound: To be great in number or amount or to be fully supplied or filled.

Admonish: advise somebody: to advise somebody to do or, more often, not to do something.

Aesop: "… an ancient and famous Black storyteller"

Aka: Also Known As.

Artefact *or* artifact: something made or given shape by man, such as a tool or a work of art, esp. an object of archaeological interest.

Myriad: a very large number of things.

Nobel Laureate: a person who has been honored for achieving distinction in a particular field or with a particular award.

Nostalgia: a bitter sweet longing for things, persons, or situations of the past or The condition of being homesick; homesickness.

Pervade: to be present throughout.

Procrastination: the practice of carrying out less urgent tasks in preference to more urgent ones, or doing more pleasurable things in place of less pleasurable ones, and thus putting off impending tasks to a later time, sometimes to the "last minute" before the deadline.

Saint: In Christianity, "saint" has a wide variety of meanings, depending on its usage and the denomination. The original Christian usage referred to any believer who is "in Christ" and in whom Christ dwells, whether in heaven or in earth. In Orthodox and Catholic teachings, all Christians in heaven are considered to be saints, but some are considered to be worthy of higher honor, emulation, or veneration, with official church recognition given to some saints through canonization or glorification.

SALVIFIC: having the intent or power to save or redeem.

Surreal: bizarre: weirdly unfamiliar, distorted, or disturbing, like the experiences in a dream or the objects or experiences depicted in surrealism.

Tori: someone of great nature, beauty, etiquette, and intelligent. Often referred to in the sense of a godlike being or a large, convex molding used at the base of columns, etc., just above the plinth (base).

Vicissitudes: a change or variation occurring in the course of something.

24/7: 24 hours seven days a week.

Some Names in this Book and their Meanings:

Adaeze: Origin is Nigerian, Igbo name meaning Princess.

Artie: Origin is American, short for Arthur (origin, welsh); Artie means "Bear."

Bernadine: Origin is French. Form of Bernard usually a name for female child. Bernard means "bold as a bear."

Charity: Origin is English. Means giving, "kindness."

Cherie: Origin is French. Means "dear."

Chioma: Origin is Nigerian, Igbo name meaning good God or good luck.

Christa: Origin is English. Means "Christ-Bearer or follower of Christ".

Charles: Origin is German. Means "free man".

Dave: Origin is English. Diminutive form of David. David, origin is Hebrew. Means "beloved".

Dawnmarie: Dawn originates from English meaning sunrise; Marie originates from French, meaning "of the sea or bitter'.

Diane: Origin is French. Means "Divine".

Donald: Origin: Scottish. Means "World Leader".

Ebisike: Origin is Nigerian, Igbo name meaning Living well.

Eboh: Origin is Nigerian, Igbo name and diminutive form of Ebomuche. Meaning Consolation.

Eucharia: From the word, Eucharist: Origin is Greek. Means "thanksgiving".

Evelyn: Origin is English. Means "beautiful bird".

Eze: Origin is Nigerian, Igbo name meaning "King".

Frances: Origin is Latin. Means "France or Free".

Hillary: Origin is Greek. Means "Cheerful".

Irene: Origin is Greek. Means "Peace."

Josephine: Origin is French. Means "God will increase".

Justina: Origin is American. Means "Just, Fair".

Jewel: Origin is English. Means "Precious Stone".

Jodie: Origin is English. "Diminutive form of names beginning with J".

Jessica: Origin is Hebrew. Means "God holds".

Mark: Origin is Latin. Means "Warlike".

Martin: Origin is Latin. Means "Servant of Mars, god of war."

Marian: Origin English. Means "bitter or from the sea".

Michael: Origin is Hebrew. Means "Who is like God?"

Nicole: Origin is French. Means "Victory of the people".

Norah: Origin is English. Means "Honor".

Rae: Origin is English. "Diminutive form of Rachel or Raymond".

Richard: Origin is English. Means "Brave Ruler".

Russell: Origin is English. Means "Red".

Stanley: Origin is English. Means "From the stony field".

Susan: Origin is Hebrew. Means "Lily".

Sue: Origin is English. Means "Lily".

Sylvester: Origin is English. Means "From the Forest".

Todd: Origin is English. Means "Fox".

Uchechukwu: Origin is Nigerian, Igbo name meaning "God's will".

Virginia: Origin is Latin. Means "Pure".

Veronica: Origin is Greek. Means "Bringing Victory".

Yvette: Origin is French. Means "Yew" (Tree).

Bibliography

Beyond the Stars Productions. (1999). Famous Last words. Retrieved July 23, 2014 from http://users.belgacom.net/gc674645/grave/lastword.html.

Brain Candy Collections. Dying words, the last words spoken by famous people at death, or shortly before. Retrieved July 23, 2014 from http://corsinet.com/braincandy/dying.html.

Frosbel. (Aug 28, 2011). Famous Atheists Last Words Before Dying. Retrieved July 23, 2014 from http://www.nairaland.com/746723/famous-atheists-last-words-before.

WORD DEFINITIONS TAKEN FROM THE FOLLOWING:

Free online dictionary. Retrieved July 23, 2014 from http://dictionary.reference.com.

Free online dictionary. Retrieved July 23, 2014 from www.Ask.com.

Free online dictionary. Retrieved July 23, 2014 from http://www.answers.com.

Free online dictionary. Retrieved July 23, 2014 from http://www.bing.com.

Free online dictionary. Retrieved July 23, 2014 from http://www.merriam-webster.com/dictionary.

Free online dictionary. Retrieved July 23, 2014 from http://www.thefreedictionary.com.

Free online dictionary. Retrieved July 23, 2014 from http://en.wikipedia.org.

Free online dictionary. Retrieved July 23, 2014 from www.yourdictionary.com

Origin and Meaning of the baby name. Retrieved July 23, 2014 from http://www.babynames.com.

September 11 attacks. Retrieved July 23, 2014 from http://en.wikipedia.org/wiki/September_11_attacks

About the Author

Frances M. Chioma Ebisike-Eboh is a wife and mother of two. She and her husband, Rev. Dr. Martins Eboh, founded All Power Heritage Ministries Inc. She is a social worker and former director at the Preventive Services of The New York Foundling, one of the oldest and largest social service agencies in the United States, where she won several service and leadership awards. Frances obtained her master's degree in social work from New York University in New York City. She was born and raised in Nigeria, West Africa, and currently lives in the United States with her husband and children.

Endorsement

"What incredible stories that will be sure to encourage you and open your eyes to the many ways God might be working in your life."

Pastor David VanDonge

Printed in the United States
By Bookmasters